ROAD FUNDS AND ROAD USER CHARGES IN THE CAREC REGION

DECEMBER 2022

 Creative Commons Attribution 3.0 IGO license (CC BY 3.0 IGO)

© 2022 Asian Development Bank
6 ADB Avenue, Mandaluyong City, 1550 Metro Manila, Philippines
Tel +63 2 8632 4444; Fax +63 2 8636 2444
www.adb.org

Some rights reserved. Published in 2022.

ISBN 978-92-9269-972-7 (print); 978-92-9269-973-4 (electronic); 978-92-9269-974-1 (ebook)
Publication Stock No. SPR220592-2
DOI: http://dx.doi.org/10.22617/SPR220592-2

The views expressed in this publication are those of the authors and do not necessarily reflect the views and policies of the Asian Development Bank (ADB) or its Board of Governors or the governments they represent.

ADB does not guarantee the accuracy of the data included in this publication and accepts no responsibility for any consequence of their use. The mention of specific companies or products of manufacturers does not imply that they are endorsed or recommended by ADB in preference to others of a similar nature that are not mentioned.

By making any designation of or reference to a particular territory or geographic area, or by using the term "country" in this document, ADB does not intend to make any judgments as to the legal or other status of any territory or area.

This work is available under the Creative Commons Attribution 3.0 IGO license (CC BY 3.0 IGO) https://creativecommons.org/licenses/by/3.0/igo/. By using the content of this publication, you agree to be bound by the terms of this license. For attribution, translations, adaptations, and permissions, please read the provisions and terms of use at https://www.adb.org/terms-use#openaccess.

This CC license does not apply to non-ADB copyright materials in this publication. If the material is attributed to another source, please contact the copyright owner or publisher of that source for permission to reproduce it. ADB cannot be held liable for any claims that arise as a result of your use of the material.

Please contact pubsmarketing@adb.org if you have questions or comments with respect to content, or if you wish to obtain copyright permission for your intended use that does not fall within these terms, or for permission to use the ADB logo.

Corrigenda to ADB publications may be found at http://www.adb.org/publications/corrigenda.

Notes:
In this publication, "$" refers to United States dollars.

On the cover: Vehicles passing through the Lahore Ring Road and the Shah Maqsood toll plaza at the Hassanabdal-Havelian Expressway in Pakistan (top photos); and the A365 Highway in the Kyrgyz Republic (middle photo). Photos by Madiha Aijaz and Nasr ur Rahman (top photos), and Serge Cartier van Dissel (middle photo).

CONTENTS

Tables and Figures	iv
Acknowledgments	vii
Abbreviations	viii
Introduction	**1**
First-Generation Road Funds	1
Second-Generation Road Funds	2
Road Funds in the Central Asia Regional Economic Cooperation Region	2
Azerbaijan	**4**
Road Fund Management	4
Road Fund Revenue	7
Kyrgyz Republic	**16**
Road Fund Management	16
Road Fund Revenue	20
Mongolia	**29**
Road Fund Management	29
Road Fund Revenue	32
Pakistan	**41**
Road Fund Management	41
Road Fund Revenue	45
Uzbekistan	**53**
Road Fund Management	53
Road Fund Revenue	59
Road Fund Management	**74**
Eligible Activities	74
Management Structure	78
Funding Approval and Allocation	80
Financial and Technical Accountability	83
Road Fund Revenue	**87**
Revenue Sources	87
Revenue Levels and Funding Needs	96

TABLES AND FIGURES

Tables

1	Activities Eligible for Financing from the Road Budget Trust Fund	5
2	Revenue Sources of the Road Budget Trust Fund	7
3	Road Tax on Fuel	8
4	Road Tax for Foreign Vehicles (US$)	8
5	Vehicle Excise Tax Rates	9
6	Vehicle Custom Duty Rates	9
7	Fees for International Road Permits	10
8	Vehicle Technical Inspection Fees	10
9	Simplified Tax Rates for Transporters	11
10	Fines on Oversized and Overweight Vehicles	11
11	Annual Budgeted Revenues of the Road Budget Trust Fund 2018–2022 (AZN)	12
12	Expenditure of the Road Budget Trust Fund for 2020 (AZN)	14
13	Activities Eligible for Financing from the Road Fund	17
14	Members of the Road Fund Supervisory Board in the Kyrgyz Republic	18
15	Competencies of the Road Fund Supervisory Board in the Kyrgyz Republic	18
16	Sources of Funding of the Road Fund (2021)	21
17	Fuel Excise Tax Rates	22
18	Vehicle Registration and Reregistration Fees (Som)	23
19	Earmarked Road User Charge Revenues 2008–2012 (Som million)	24
20	Republican Budget Allocations to Road Maintenance and Repair	25
21	Earmarked Revenues in 2018	26
22	National Budget Allocations to Roads (Som million)	26
23	Calculation of Maintenance and Repair Needs by the Ministry of Transport and Communications	28
24	Activities Eligible for Financing from the State Road Fund	30
25	Sources of Funding of the State Road Fund	32
26	Vehicle Excise Tax (MNT)	33
27	Tax on Gasoline and Diesel	34
28	Toll Rates	34
29	Annual Revenues of the State Road Fund 2014–2020 (MNT million)	36
30	Annual Expenditure of the State Road Fund 2014–2020 (MNT million)	38
31	Maintenance and Repair Needs (MNT million)	40

32	Activities Eligible for Financing from the Road Maintenance Account	42
33	Members of the National Highway Authority and the Road Maintenance Account Management Entities	43
34	Sources of Funding of the Road Maintenance Account	46
35	Motorway Toll Rates (US$/km)	47
36	Actual Revenues of the Road Maintenance Account 2014–2021 (PRs million)	48
37	Annual Planned Expenditure of the Road Maintenance Account 2017–2021 (PRs million)	49
38	Maintenance Needs and Approved Plans	51
39	Activities Eligible for Financing from the Republican Road Fund and Subsequent Republican Fund	55
40	Sources of Funding of the Republican Road Fund	60
41	Sources of Funding of the Republican and Regional Trust Funds for Road Development	61
42	Vehicle Registration Fee for Used Vehicles (% of minimum wage for each horsepower)	61
43	Foreign Vehicle Entry Fees (US$ per vehicle)	62
44	Vehicle Customs Duty for 2019 (US$)	63
45	Fuel Consumption Excise Tax (SUM/liter or SUM/cubic meter)	63
46	Fuel Excise Tax (SUM per ton, %)	64
47	Annual Revenues of the Republican Road Fund 2013–2018 (SUM billion)	65
48	Annual Budgets of the Ministry of Transport (SUM billion)	66
49	Estimated Fuel Production Excise Tax Revenue (2020)	67
50	Estimated Fuel Consumption Excise Tax Revenue (2020)	67
51	Expenditure of the Republican Road Fund (SUM billion)	68
52	Expenditure by Uzavtoyul, State Committee for Roads, and Committee for Roads (SUM billion)	70
53	Expenditure on Current Repair and Maintenance (SUM billion)	71
54	Budget Allocations from the Republican Fund in 2022 (SUM billion)	72
55	Activities Eligible for Financing from the Road Funds in the Central Asia Regional Economic Cooperation Region	74
56	Road Fund Management in the Central Asia Regional Economic Cooperation Region	79
57	Types of Road Fund Accounts	83
58	Lapsable and Non-lapsable Road Fund Accounts	83
59	On- and Off-Budget Road Fund Revenues	84
60	Auditing and Reporting of Road Fund Activities	86
61	Revenue Sources of Road Funds (%)	87
62	Fuel Tax Rates (US$/liter)	90
63	Imported Vehicle Taxes, Duties, and Fees (US$/vehicle)	92
64	Road Fund Revenues and Funding Needs	97

Figures

1	Management Structure of the Road Budget Trust Fund in Azerbaijan	5
2	Annual Budgeted Revenues of the Road Budget Trust Fund 2011–2022 (US$ million)	13
3	Management Structure of the Road Fund in the Kyrgyz Republic	19
4	Annual Allocations from the Republican Budget 2018–2022 (US$ million)	27
5	Management Structure of the State Road Fund in Mongolia	31
6	Annual Revenues of the State Road Fund 2014–2020 (US$ million)	37
7	Annual Expenditure of the State Road Fund 2014–2020 (US$ million)	38
8	Management Structure of the Road Maintenance Account in Pakistan	44
9	Annual Revenues of the Road Maintenance Account 2014–2021 (US$ million)	48
10	Annual Planned Expenditure of the Road Maintenance Account 2017–2021 (US$ million)	50
11	Maintenance Needs and Approved Plans (US$ million)	52
12	Management Structure of the Republican Road Fund in Uzbekistan (before 2019)	56
13	Management Structure of the Republican Fund in Uzbekistan (after 2019)	57
14	Annual Revenues of the Republican Road Fund 2013–2018 (US$ million)	66
15	Annual Expenditure of the Republican Road Fund (US$ million)	69
16	Expenditure by Uzavtoyul, State Committee for Roads, and Committee for Roads (US$ million)	70
17	Expenditure by Uzavtoyul, State Committee for Roads, and Committee for Roads (US$ million)	71
18	Possible Setup of the Road Fund Secretariat and Board	80
19	Revenue Sources of Road Funds (%)	88
20	Fuel Tax Rates (US$/liter)	90
21	Road Fund Revenues and Funding Needs (US$/km)	97

ACKNOWLEDGMENTS

This publication on road funds and road user charges in the Central Asia Regional Economic Cooperation (CAREC) region was developed as part of the support of the CAREC Program toward the establishment of competitive transport corridors; facilitation of movement of people and goods; and provision of sustainable, safe, and user-friendly transport and trade networks. This publication was prepared in the context of CAREC's Transport Strategy 2030 and aims to improve the financing, management, and maintenance of CAREC road corridors through the sharing of best practices that exist within CAREC countries regarding road funds and the earmarking of road user charges.

This publication was prepared by Serge Cartier van Dissel, road management consultant for the Asian Development Bank (ADB). Thanks go to the different people who contributed information on the experiences with road funds and road user charges in the various CAREC countries. Special thanks go to Thomas Herz, Michael Anyala, Ritu Mishra, and Pilar Sahilan (consultant) of ADB for their contributions to and detailed review of the various versions of this document. Last but certainly not the least, the contributions received from the staff of the different road agencies and ADB resident missions in CAREC countries must be recognized—those who provided detailed information on the experiences with road funds and road user charges in their respective countries; who participated in discussions on these topics; and who assisted in the review of this document, and corrected and complemented the information where necessary.

ABBREVIATIONS

ADB	Asian Development Bank
AMP	Annual Maintenance Plan (Pakistan)
CAREC	Central Asia Regional Economic Cooperation
cc	cubic centimeter
COVID-19	coronavirus disease
HDM4	Highway Design and Management version 4
km	kilometer
MOC	Ministry of Communications (Pakistan)
MOT	Ministry of Transport (Azerbaijan and Uzbekistan)
MOTC	Ministry of Transport and Communications (Kyrgyz Republic)
MRTD	Ministry of Roads and Transport Development (Mongolia)
NHA	National Highway Authority (Pakistan)
NHMP	National Highway and Motorway Police (Pakistan)
NTRC	National Transport Research Centre (Pakistan)
PPP	public–private partnership
RAMD	Road Asset Management Division (Pakistan)
RAMS	road asset management system
RMA	Road Maintenance Account (Pakistan)
RMD	Road Maintenance Department (Kyrgyz Republic and Mongolia)
RRF	Republican Road Fund (Uzbekistan)
RTDC	Road and Transport Development Centre (Mongolia)
SOP	standard operating procedure
SUE	state unitary enterprise
US	United States

INTRODUCTION

Traditionally, road sector financing in developing countries comes from general budget allocations of a national or local government. Budget allocations to the road sector depend strongly on the total available budget for the year concerned, as well as budget needs in other sectors such as health, education, defense, etc. As a result, budget allocations to the road sector tend to vary from one year to the next, with underfunding tending to be the norm. Especially road maintenance is often underfunded, causing maintenance backlogs and leading to accelerated deterioration of the road network and the need for costly rehabilitation or reconstruction. To address the underfunding and its variability, countries around the world have introduced road funds. Generally, these road funds receive funding from hypothecated or earmarked road user charge revenues. Road user charges refer to taxes and fees that are paid specifically by road users, and may include fuel taxes or levies, vehicle import duties or taxes, road tolls, vehicle technical inspection fees, etc. The earmarking of these road user charges to a road fund introduces a "user pays" principle where road users finance the operation and maintenance of the road network that they make use of. Although road funds may also contribute to road construction and improvement costs, generally, the road fund revenues are insufficient to cover such costs. Therefore, road funds tend to limit themselves to financing the maintenance and, to a certain degree, also the rehabilitation of the road network. Although road funds have remained largely the same in the way that they are financed and the activities that they fund, their management and governance have evolved over time. Distinction is often made between first-generation road funds that focused on earmarking road user charges, and second-generation road funds where greater attention is given to the management of the road fund.

First-Generation Road Funds

The first-generation road funds are often dedicated treasury accounts under the Ministry of Finance, which are designated specifically for financing certain activities in the road sector. The main objective of these first-generation road funds is to earmark road user charge revenues for the road sector. This has the objective of making the funding levels more stable and predictable from one year to the next. The dedicated treasury accounts often allow unused funds to be carried over to the next year, facilitating the planning of works to fit the seasons and avoiding any loss of funds because of delays in procurement or implementation. These first-generation road funds tend to be established through simple legislation (e.g., presidential decrees) linked to existing laws related to the budget or to special funds. The earmarked road user charge revenues form part of the general budget. The first-generation road funds are often managed directly by the government department or agency that is responsible for managing the road network and for implementing the roadworks (either directly or through contractors). Use of funds follows general government financial procedures, with limited reporting and accounting requirements. Independent financial audits are uncommon, and technical audits of ongoing and completed works (quality and quantity) are generally

> **The main objective of the first-generation road funds is to earmark road user charge revenues for the road sector.**

not carried out. Transparency is also limited, with little to no participation of road users in setting priorities or monitoring progress. Often, this has resulted in strong political interference and extensive use of funds for unauthorized expenditures.

Second-Generation Road Funds

This led to the creation of the so-called second-generation road funds. The main objective of the second-generation road funds is to improve accountability and transparency in the use of earmarked revenues. This often includes the creation of a separate entity to manage the road fund, as part of the overall commercialization of the road sector. This consists of a secretariat for the day-to-day running of the fund, and a Supervisory Board to approve the use of funds and decide on the rates to be applied for earmarked road user charges in response to funding needs of the road network. The Supervisory Board includes representatives of different government entities, and often also includes road user representatives (e.g., transporters' association). Therefore, the management of the road fund is separated from the implementation of the roadworks. The establishment of the road fund is generally through a specific law and is often complemented by regulations governing the operation of the road fund. Some earmarked road user charge revenues are extra-budgetary, further ensuring the predictability of funding. Reporting and accounting procedures are strengthened, requiring independent financial audits every year and regular technical audits, as well as annual publication of the audits together with a detailed annual report on the use of the road fund, greatly increasing transparency.

The main objective of the second-generation road funds is to improve accountability and transparency in the use of earmarked revenues.

Road Funds in the Central Asia Regional Economic Cooperation Region

The Central Asia Regional Economic Cooperation (CAREC) region has seen a large variety of road funds. In the former Soviet countries, road funds were created in the late 1990s after the Soviet Union fell apart and insufficient funding was available for the road sector. Many of these have since been abolished or have transformed over time. Functioning road funds currently exist in five CAREC member countries: Azerbaijan, the Kyrgyz Republic, Mongolia, Pakistan, and Uzbekistan.[1] A review of these road funds shows that they cannot be easily qualified as either first-generation or second-generation road funds, and actually contain elements of both models.

---

[1] Currently, other CAREC member countries do not have functioning road funds. Georgia, Kazakhstan, Tajikistan, and Turkmenistan established road funds in the 1990s, but these were abolished in the early 2000s as part of the economic reform supported by the International Monetary Fund. Although these countries continue to collect road user charges, the revenues are not earmarked for the road sector and remain in the national or local budget. Tajikistan is currently working on the establishment of a road maintenance fund, but this is still in the design stage. In the People's Republic of China, a maintenance fee used to be collected at county and prefecture levels that was earmarked for local road maintenance, but this was replaced by a fuel tax that is currently collected at the central level. Currently, vehicle purchase tax and fuel tax revenues are used to finance the road sector, but these revenues are not earmarked, and a road fund was never established.

This document will look at the road funds in these countries in more detail. The initial chapters will describe the road funds in these five countries in detail, including their history and current operation. The final two chapters will examine in more detail the institutional aspects and operational procedures of the road funds in the CAREC region, and the road user charge revenues that finance them, drawing lessons for the introduction and continued development of road funds in the region and beyond.

AZERBAIJAN

Azerbaijan has a public road network of 17,755 kilometers (km), including 1,653 km of magistral roads; 2,884 km of republican roads; and 13,218 km of collector and local roads. The management of the public road network is the responsibility of the State Agency for Azerbaijan Automobile Roads (AAYDA).[2] Maintenance and repair of the public roads are carried out by the 106 economic societies under AAYDA, including 7 corridor-based motorway maintenance societies, 8 societies for maintenance of highways around Baku, 21 specialized road maintenance societies, 54 district-based road maintenance societies, 12 landscaping societies, and 4 other societies. Other roadworks are contracted out to private sector contractors.

Road Fund Management

A Road Budget Trust Fund was created in 2006 through Presidential Order #1729 "on establishment of the Road Budget Trust Fund within the State Budget of the Republic of Azerbaijan," becoming effective from 1 January 2007. The Road Budget Trust Fund was created in accordance with the 2002 Law #358 "on the Budget System" that allows trust funds to be established as part of the state budget. Receipts and expenditures of such trust funds are shown separately in the state budget. Funding is restricted to defined purposes, and unused funding can be carried over to the following year. Regulations for the Road Budget Trust Fund were issued in 2007 through Decree #13 of the Cabinet of Ministers "on approval of the Rules for Spending the Funds of the Road Budget Trust Fund for the Maintenance and Repair of Public Roads of National and Local significance in the Country." The presidential order and subsequent decree serve primarily to identify the sources of funding of the Road Budget Trust Fund, and they contain very limited guidance on the management and structure of the road fund.

Eligible Activities

The 2007 Decree #13 of the Cabinet of Ministers defines that the Road Budget Trust Fund may be used only to finance the maintenance and repair of public roads. In the Law on Roads, maintenance is defined to include summer and winter maintenance (excluding pavement or structure repairs), while for repairs distinction is made between current repairs (routine pavement and structure repairs), midterm repairs (periodic maintenance), and capital repairs (rehabilitation). Reconstruction (changes to geometry) and new construction are not included under repair and cannot be financed from the Road Budget Trust Fund. Inspections and the collection of data for the road network are also not expressly mentioned as an eligible activity, although it can be considered to be included under the operation of the road network.

---

[2] Azərbaycan Avtomobil Yolları Dövlət Agentliyi (AzərAvtoYol).

Table 1: Activities Eligible for Financing from the Road Budget Trust Fund

- Summer and winter maintenance
- Current repairs
- Midterm repairs
- Capital repairs
- Operational costs

Source: Decree #13, 2007.

Management Structure

Although the Ministry of Transport (MOT) was appointed originally to manage the Road Budget Trust Fund, in 2016 this was amended through Presidential Order #2227 and AAYDA was made responsible for the management of the Road Budget Trust Fund and provides the secretariat for the road fund. There is no independent entity created to manage the Road Budget Trust Fund, and day-to-day management of the fund is by the same entity that is responsible for implementation of the works financed by the fund. There is no road fund board with representatives of other ministries or road users responsible for the management of the Road Budget Trust Fund. The role of the road fund board is played by the Ministry of Finance, which has to approve the annual work plan. The management structure of the Road Budget Trust Fund is presented in Figure 1.

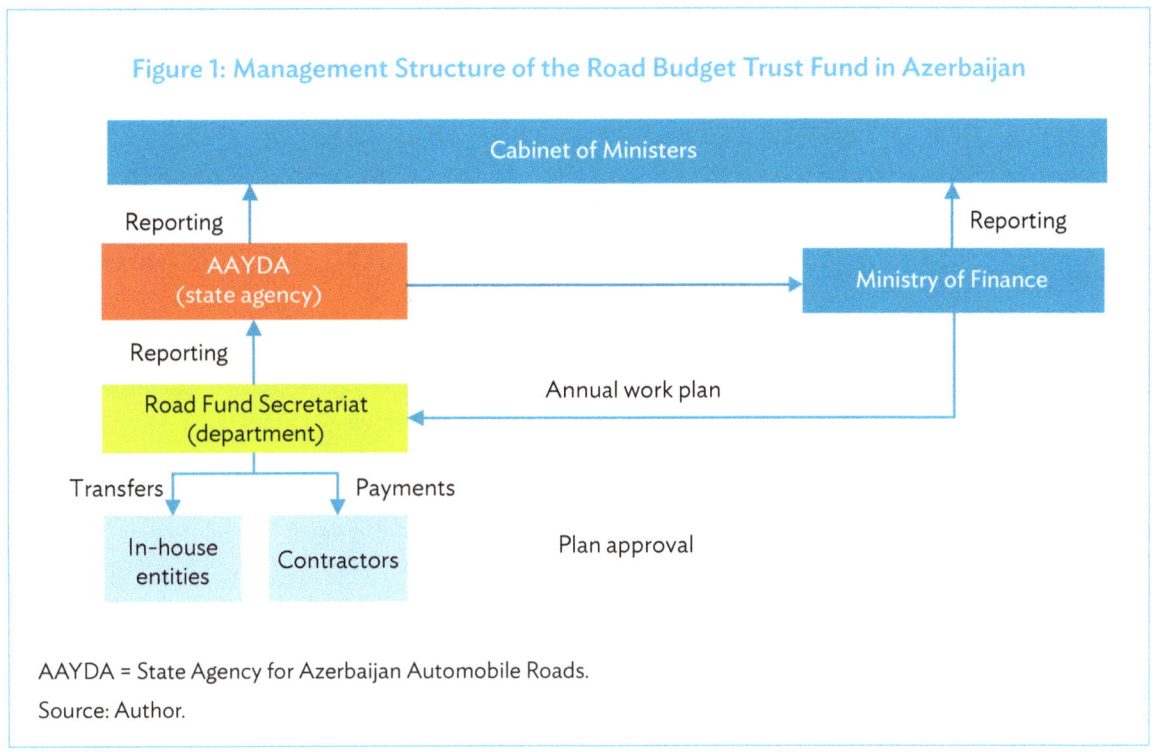

Figure 1: Management Structure of the Road Budget Trust Fund in Azerbaijan

AAYDA = State Agency for Azerbaijan Automobile Roads.
Source: Author.

Funding Approval and Allocation

The annual work plan is prepared by AAYDA and submitted to the Road Budget Trust Fund that is managed by AAYDA. Although AAYDA provides the secretariat for the Road Budget Trust Fund, the work plan and its funding require approval by the Ministry of Finance. Once approved, the funding is transferred to AAYDA as would be the case with allocations from the state budget. AAYDA is subsequently responsible for implementation within the limits of the allocated annual work plan and budget.

Financial and Technical Accountability

The Road Budget Trust Fund is set up as a special treasury account under the Ministry of Finance, with road fund revenues and expenditures reported separately from the general budget in the state budget. Decree #13 defines that AAYDA has to submit quarterly and annual reports on the Road Budget Trust Fund expenditure to the Ministry of Finance. Expenditure has to be within the limits of the actual revenue collection and in accordance with the eligible activities that may be financed by the Road Budget Trust Fund, and has to comply with general rules regarding expenditure by departments, enterprises, and organizations financed from the state budget.

The Budget Code requires that the Road Budget Trust Fund submits annual reports on revenue and expenditure to the Chamber of Accounts and to the *Milli Majilis* (Parliament). The Chamber of Accounts will provide an opinion on the annual report. The Chamber of Accounts may also carry out audits, including (i) a financial audit (determination of compliance, accuracy, integrity, and completeness of financial transactions and reports; assessment of financial management, internal control, and related information systems); (ii) a performance audit (determination of cost-effectiveness, efficiency and effectiveness of software, project, activity, operation, management and information systems), and/or (iii) a compliance audit (determination of the status of compliance with the requirements of existing legal acts by the objects of external state financial control). However, because of the limited staff of the Chamber of Audits, such audits of the Road Budget Trust Fund are not carried out each year. Audit results are published in the annual budget audit covering the entire state budget (whereby the audits will include only certain government entities, and the Road Budget Trust Fund will only be included in certain years).

The last audit of the Road Budget Trust Fund by the Chamber of Accounts was carried out in 2020 and the main findings were published in the 2020 budget audit, identifying (i) actual itemized revenue and expenditure levels; and (ii) issues with revenue predictions, estimated versus actual unit costs, allocation of funds to different parts of the country, and use of staff and equipment of the economic societies in capital works that were financed by the Road Budget Trust Fund (which cannot finance capital works). Although such audits by the Chamber of Accounts appear to be properly carried out, they are infrequent, and the full details are not published.

Road Fund Revenue

The Government of Azerbaijan collects revenues from different road user charges, several of which are earmarked for the Road Budget Trust Fund and directly finance road maintenance and repair. There are also other road user charges that are not earmarked for the Road Budget Trust Fund.

Revenue Sources

Presidential Order #1729 and the subsequent Regulations issued by the Cabinet of Ministers identify the following sources of revenue for the Road Budget Trust Fund. This includes a road tax[3] that consists of a specific road tax on fuel and a road tax on foreign vehicles, which are included together under the heading of "road tax" in the annual budget. Although the Law on Roads allows for tolls to be collected, these are not earmarked for the Road Budget Trust Fund and are instead allocated to the entity in charge of operation and maintenance of the toll road, and applied to the specific road where the tolls are collected.

Table 2: Revenue Sources of the Road Budget Trust Fund

- Road tax
  - Road tax on fuel
  - Road tax on foreign vehicles
- Vehicle customs duty
- Vehicle excise tax
- Fee for international road transport permit
- Fee for vehicle technical inspection
- Simplified tax for cargo and passenger transporters
- Fines on overweight/oversized vehicles
- State budget allocations

Source: Presidential Order #1729 on establishment of the Road Budget Trust Fund within the State Budget, 2006.

Road tax on fuel. The road tax on fuel is regulated in the Tax Code. It is a special tax charged for fuel produced in Azerbaijan or imported into the country. In the case of domestic production, a tax of AZN0.02 per liter is levied in addition to the value-added tax and a fuel excise tax and applied to the wholesale price and collected by the State Tax Service. In the case of imported fuel, the tax is collected by the State Customs Committee upon entry into the country. The road tax on fuel is set at AZN0.02 per liter (equivalent to 1.2 US dollar cents per liter) and applies to all fuel types (gasoline, diesel, and liquid gas).

---

[3] This should not be confused with the road tax applied in many other former Soviet countries, which refers to a corporate turnover tax.

Table 3: Road Tax on Fuel

Production/Import	Fuel Type	Rate (AZN)	Rate (US$)
Domestic production	Gasoline, diesel, natural gas	AZN0.02 per liter	$0.012 per liter
Imported fuel	Gasoline, diesel, natural gas	AZN0.02 per liter	$0.012 per liter

Source: Tax Code, 2021.

This road tax on fuel is different from the excise tax on fuel that is also collected in Azerbaijan. The excise tax on fuel is also regulated by the Tax Code, with excise rates set in the 2001 Resolution #20 of the Cabinet of Ministers "on approval of excise tax rates on goods imported into the territory of the Republic of Azerbaijan." The fuel excise rate varies from AZN80 to AZN200 per ton, depending on the fuel type and octane level. This is equivalent to about $0.04–$0.09 per liter, 3–7 times as high as the road tax on fuel. However, the fuel excise tax is not earmarked for the Road Budget Trust Fund and remains in the state budget.

Road tax on foreign vehicles. This fee is paid by foreign vehicles that enter the territory of Azerbaijan and is regulated in the Tax Code. The fee is paid when a foreign vehicle enters or leaves the country and is collected by the State Customs Committee and earmarked for the State Road Fund. The rate is set in United States (US) dollars and depends on the type and size of vehicle as well as the duration of stay in the country. In addition to the entry fees listed below, heavy foreign freight vehicles have to pay an additional fee per kilometer (km) driven in Azerbaijan, ranging from $0.15/km for vehicles weighing 38–41 tons, to $1.8/km for vehicles weighing more than 81 tons. This tax is for foreign vehicle entry and is different from the fee for the international road transport permit that is charged to foreign carriers that transport goods or passengers in Azerbaijan (see further down).

Table 4: Road Tax for Foreign Vehicles
(US$)

Stay Duration	Cars			Buses			Trucks	
	<2,000 cc	2,000–4,000 cc	>4,000 cc	<12 seats	13–30 seats	>31 seats	≤4 axles	>4 axles
1 day				$15	$20	$25	$20	$30
Up to 1 week				$30	$40	$50		
Up to 2 weeks							$40	$80
Up to 1 month	$15	$20	$40	$100	$140	$175	$140	$280
Up to 3 months	$30	$40	$60	$300	$400	$500	$400	$800
Up to 1 year	$40	$80	$120	$1,050	$1,400	$1,750	$1,400	$2,800
Per day over 1 year	$0.5	$0.6	$1.2	$12	$15	$20	$15	$30

cc = cubic centimeter.
Source: Tax Code, 2021.

Vehicle excise tax. The excise tax on imported vehicles is regulated by the Tax Code. The tax is paid when a vehicle is imported into the country, and is collected by the State Customs Committee. The tax rate depends on the type of vehicle and the engine size, with rates defined per cubic centimeter (cc) of engine capacity and increasing for larger engines. The rates of the new 2022 Tax Code are indicated in Table 5. For buses over 1 year old or having driven more than 100,000 km, the vehicle excise tax is increased by 50%. For cars with engines of over 3,000 cc and older than 3 years, the rate is increased by about 15%. For all cars older than 7 years, the rate is increased by 20% for gasoline vehicles and 50% for diesel vehicles. In 2020, a total of 53,577 vehicles were reported to have been imported into Azerbaijan, up from 47,483 in 2019.

Table 5: Vehicle Excise Tax Rates

Vehicle type	Engine Size	Tax Rate	US$ per Vehicle
Car	<2,000 cc	AZN0.3/cc	<$350
	2,001–3,000 cc	AZN600 + AZN/cc over 2,000 cc	$350–$3,300
	3,001–4,000 cc	AZN5,600 + AZN13.0/cc over 3,000 cc	$3,300–$11,000
	4,001–5,000 cc	AZN18,600 + AZN35.0/cc over 4,000 cc	$11,000–$31,500
	>5,000 cc	AZN53,600 + AZN70.0/cc over 5,000 cc	>$31,500
Bus	<4,000 cc	AZN2.0/cc	<$4,700
	4,001–6,000 cc	AZN8,000 + AZN4.0/cc over 4,000 cc	$4,700–$9,400
	6,001–8,000 cc	AZN16,000 + AZN6.0/cc over 6,000 cc	$9,400–$16,500
	8,001–10,000 cc	AZN28,000 + AZN8.0/cc over 8,000 cc	$16,500–$25,900
	>10,000 cc	AZN44,000 + AZN10.0/cc over 10,000 cc	>$25,900

cc = cubic centimeter.
Source: Tax Code, 2022

Vehicle customs duty. The vehicle customs duty is collected by the State Customs Committee together with the vehicle excise tax when the vehicle is imported into Azerbaijan. For passenger cars and buses with internal combustion engines (petrol, diesel, and hybrid engines), the rate is based on the engine capacity, with a rate of AZN1.19/cc ($0.70/cc). For fully electric passenger cars, the rate is based on the customs value of the car, with a uniform tax rate of 15% of the value.

Table 6: Vehicle Custom Duty Rates

Vehicle Type	Engine Type	Tax Rate	US$ per Vehicle
Car	Combustion	AZN1.19/cc	$0.7/cc
	Electric	15% of customs value	15% of customs value
Bus	Combustion	AZN1.19/cc	$0.7/cc

cc = cubic centimeter.
Source: State Customs Service website, January 2022.

Fee for international road transport permit. The permit for international road transport is regulated by the 1996 Decree #141 and by the 1997 Decree #6 of the Cabinet of Ministers "on approval of the Regulations on the Permit System regulating international road transport in the territory of the Republic of Azerbaijan." According to these regulations, foreign transporters of goods or passengers have to acquire a permit for international road transport in Azerbaijan. The system includes quota agreements with different countries regarding the number of permits that may be issued. These permits are valid for 1 month and allow the transporter to unload, load, or transit cargo or passengers. The fees are paid in US dollars to the State Customs Service upon entry into the country. The rates are set in the 2001 Law #223 "on State Duties" and are presented in Table 7.

Table 7: Fees for International Road Permits

Transport Type	Transporter Type	Vehicle Type	Fee (US$)
Entry/exit and transit	For Azerbaijan transporters to other countries	Trucks	$20 per permit
		Buses	$10 per permit
	For transporters from countries with intergovernmental agreements	Trucks	$100 per permit
		Buses	$50 per permit
	For transporters from countries without intergovernmental agreements	Trucks	$150 per permit
		Buses	$75 per permit
Loading of foreign vehicles in Azerbaijan			$100 per permit
Shipments to and from a third country			$600 per permit
Entry of foreign vehicles without cargo		Trucks	$350 per permit
		Buses	$80 per permit
Heavy foreign vehicle entry into Baku, Sumgayit, and Ganja			$25 per permit
Violation of intergovernmental agreements (exceeding quota)			$400 per permit

cc = cubic centimeter.
Source: Law #223 on State Duties, 2001.

Fee for vehicle technical inspections. The fee for vehicle technical inspections is regulated by the 1998 Law #517 "on Traffic," while the rates are set in the 2002 Law #223 "on State Duties." The fee is paid not only for annual vehicle technical inspections, but also for inspections carried out with respect to the import of vehicles. The technical inspections are carried out and the fees are collected by the Main Traffic Police Department under the Ministry of Internal Affairs. The rates are provided in Table 8.

Table 8: Vehicle Technical Inspection Fees

Vehicle Type	Fee (AZN)	Fee (US$)
Vehicles	AZN30	$17.6
Motorcycles, tractors, construction vehicles, trailers, semi-trailers	AZN15	$8.8

Source: Law on State Duties, 2002.

Simplified tax for transporters. The simplified tax for transporters is regulated in the Tax Code. It is paid on a monthly basis by the owner of the vehicle based on the type and size of vehicle, and it is collected by the State Tax Service. The rates of the new 2022 Tax Code are indicated in Table 9. Rates are increased by 50% for vehicles operating in or from the cities of Sumgayit, Ganja, and Absheron and by 100% for vehicles operating in or from the capital Baku.

Table 9: Simplified Tax Rates for Transporters

Type of Vehicle	Rate per Month (AZN)	Rate per Month (US$)
Taxi	AZN9.0 per vehicle	$5.29 per vehicle
Bus	AZN1.8 per seat	$1.06 per seat
Truck	AZN1.0 per ton capacity	$0.59 per ton capacity

Source: Tax Code, 2022.

Fines on overweight and/or oversized vehicles. The fines for oversized and/or overweight vehicles are regulated by the Code of Administrative Offences (Law #96 of 2015). The rates depend on the type of offense and are doubled in the case of a repeat offense of the same type in the same year. The fines are issued and collected by the Main Traffic Police Department under the Ministry of Internal Affairs.

Table 10: Fines on Oversized and Overweight Vehicles

Type of Offense	Owner	Rate (AZN)	Rate (US$)
Oversized vehicle	Individual	AZN200	$118
Overweight vehicle	Individual	AZN600	$352
Overweight and oversized vehicle	Individual	AZN1,400–AZN1,700	$824–$1,000
Overweight and/or oversized vehicle	Entity	AZN4,000–AZN5,000	$2,353–$2,941

Source: Code of Administrative Offences, 2015.

Revenue Levels

The revenue levels as included in the annual budget are shown in Table 11 for the past 5 years (2018–2022). For 2020, this also includes the actual revenue levels as reported by the Chamber of Accounts in the budget audit for that year. In the period from 2018 to 2022, budgeted revenues from road user charges have increased from AZN200 million ($119 million) to just under AZN310 million ($182 million). State budget allocations have reduced over time and no longer form part of the revenue of the Road Budget Trust Fund. The road tax, especially on fuel, forms the main source of funding, but this portion was reduced from a maximum of 49% of total revenue in 2019 to only 38% in the 2022 budget (this is at least partly because of the coronavirus disease [COVID-19] pandemic and reduced fuel consumption). This is followed by the customs duty on imported vehicles and, to a lesser extent, the excise tax on imported vehicles, which are providing an increasing percentage of total revenue. Together, these three sources currently provide 83% of the total revenue of the Road Budget Trust Fund.

Table 11: Annual Budgeted Revenues of the Road Budget Trust Fund 2018–2022 (AZN)

Source	2018 Budget	2019 Budget	2020 Budget	2020 Actual	2021 Budget	2022 Budget
Road tax	91,000,000	114,000,000	121,000,000	104,858,100	114,000,000	116,500,000
Vehicle customs duty	41,000,000	50,000,000	90,400,000	131,379,500	91,000,000	89,500,000
Vehicle excise tax	30,000,000	31,000,000	50,000,000	47,788,100	46,000,000	50,000,000
Foreign vehicle permit	15,000,000	15,600,000	16,000,000	14,471,100	15,500,000	15,500,000
Vehicle technical inspection	16,000,000	16,200,000	15,600,000	18,178,400	17,500,000	22,500,000
Simplified tax transporters	7,000,000	7,000,000	7,000,000	5,570,300	6,000,000	6,000,000
Other						9,865,000
Subtotal	**200,000,000**	**233,800,000**	**300,000,000**	**322,245,500**	**290,000,000**	**309,865,000**
State budget allocation	133,000,000	88,200,000	22,000,000			
Total AZN	**333,000,000**	**322,000,000**	**322,000,000**	**322,245,500**	**290,000,000**	**309,865,000**
Exchange rate US$1	1.68480	1.69725	1.70000	1.70000	1.70000	1.70000
Total US$ million	**$197.6**	**$189.7**	**$189.4**	**$189.6**	**$170.6**	**$182.3**

Source: State Budget of the Republic of Azerbaijan 2018–2022, Ministry of Finance.

Figure 2 shows the budgeted annual revenue from the different sources in US dollars for the period 2011–2022, including the actual revenues as reported by the Chamber of Accounts in the 2020 budget audit. The big dip in revenue in 2016–2017 was the result of a devaluation of the Azerbaijan manat from roughly AZN0.8 per dollar up to 2015 to nearly AZN1.8 per dollar in 2017. Since the middle of 2019, the exchange rate has been fixed at AZN1.7 per dollar. In US dollar terms, the revenue levels are increasing and reached $182 million in 2022, but have still not reached the 2011 levels of $213 million.

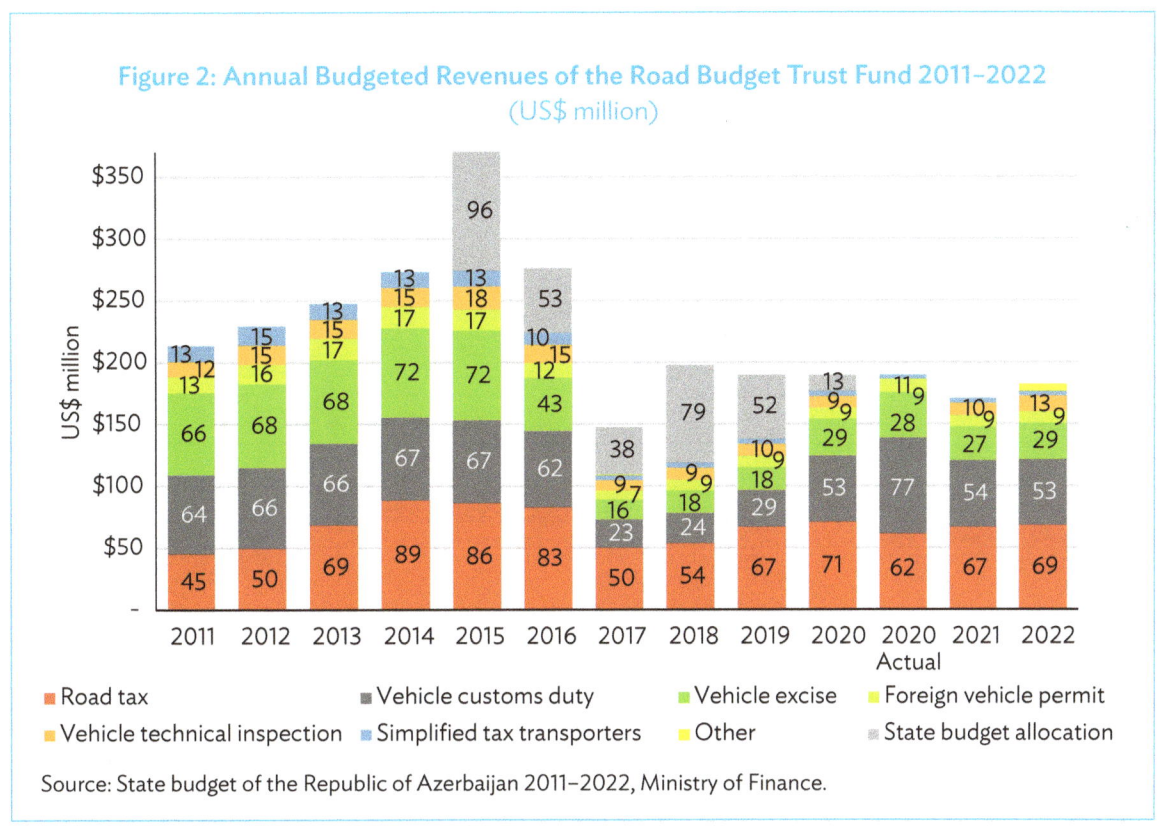

Figure 2: Annual Budgeted Revenues of the Road Budget Trust Fund 2011–2022 (US$ million)

Source: State budget of the Republic of Azerbaijan 2011–2022, Ministry of Finance.

Revenue Allocation

The Road Budget Trust Fund is used only for financing maintenance and repair activities of magistral, republican, and local roads, with minor allocations to operational costs. This is implemented by the 103 economic societies under AAYDA. These are funded under different budget lines and expenditure is organized by type of input (labor, materials, equipment, etc.) rather than by type of output (routine maintenance, current repair, midterm repair) as would be the case where works are carried out on a contract basis. This information is not published except when an audit is carried out by the Chamber of Accounts. The audit carried out in 2020 shows that one-third of the expenditure involves staff salaries, mainly for the 103 economic societies responsible for carrying out maintenance and repair works and, together with the 2% in utility costs, form a relatively fixed cost that is independent of the amount of work carried out. The audit also reports that the staff and equipment of the economic societies were used in construction works, despite being paid from the Road Budget Trust Fund that is only to be used for maintenance and repair (this is one of the issues raised by the auditors). The materials for the repair works make up 45% of the expenditure and, together with the 9% of implementation related costs, make up the flexible portion of the expenditure that will vary according to needs and the available budget. The final 11% of the expenditure is related to financing costs, especially the repayment of interest and principal from loans from domestic and foreign banks (it is not clear what types of activities were financed with these loans). The expenditure for 2020 is shown in Table 12.

Table 12: Expenditure of the Road Budget Trust Fund for 2020
(AZN)

Expenditure Item		2020
Materials	Materials and services	134,870,300
Salaries	Salaries	99,856,300
Implementation	Administration and fuel	14,220,600
	Equipment	6,254,400
	Road safety	5,200,600
	Travel expenses	1,087,600
	Transport services	794,000
Financing costs	Loan repayment	29,753,600
	Banking	2,040,900
Utility costs	Electricity	2,104,300
	Natural gas	1,612,300
	Water	585,600
	Sewerage	395,100
	Communication	316,800
	Other	907,600
Total		**300,000,000**

Source: Annual Report on Execution of the State Budget of the Republic of Azerbaijan for 2020, Chamber of Accounts.

Funding Needs

A Highway Design and Management (HDM4) analysis carried out in 2010 found that an optimal budget of $288 million was required for the first 5 years to address the maintenance backlog, followed by $136 million per year for the following 15 years, allowing 88% of the network to be brought to good or fair condition by 2030. The existing budget for maintenance and rehabilitation of $243 million in 2009 ($181 million from the Road Budget Trust Fund and $62 million from the state budget) was largely in line with the identified needs. The study concluded that the amount of funding for maintenance and repair could be considered appropriate, but that allocation needed to be improved, giving higher priority to midterm repair and to maintenance and repair of roads in good to fair condition.

Road user charge revenues of the Road Budget Trust Fund have continued to increase since then in Azerbaijan manat terms, but in US dollar terms the revenue level is currently at the same level as in 2009, primarily because of the devaluation of the Azerbaijan manat in 2017. At the same time, allocations from the state budget are no longer provided, reducing the available funding to only $182 million in 2022. A significant portion of the maintenance and repair backlog has been addressed in previous years, and, therefore, funding needs should be based on the long-term maintenance and repair needs estimated at $136 million per year in 2010. However, maintenance and repair costs have increased since then. Assuming an annual increase in prices of 4%, the maintenance and repair funding needs for 2020 would be in the order of $200 million, which is largely in line with the available funding. The 2010 conclusion on the suitability of funding levels appears to still be valid, but so does the recommendation on improving the allocation of the available funding to midterm repair and to roads in good and fair condition. AAYDA have indicated that they require additional funding and have requested the Ministry of Finance to increase road user charge rates by 30%. Although Azerbaijan developed a comprehensive road asset management system (RAMS) in 2012, this does not appear to be used in a structured manner to prepare the annual plans financed by the Road Budget Trust Fund, and funding is not used efficiently. The 2010 analysis of funding needs should be updated to verify the suitability of the revenues of the Road Budget Trust Fund, and to assess the efficiency of funding allocations.

KYRGYZ REPUBLIC

The Kyrgyz Republic has a public road network of 18,942 km, including 4,219 km of international roads, 5,616 km of national roads, and 9,107 km of local roads. The Ministry of Transport and Communications (MOTC) is responsible for the public road network, with management delegated to the Road Maintenance Department (RMD)[4] that is set up as a separate legal entity under MOTC. Until recently, RMD was supported by four oblast-based regional offices (formerly PLUADs),[5] four corridor-based UADs,[6] and one state directorate responsible for the main Bishkek–Osh road, all set up as independent legal entities under MOTC. Implementation of road maintenance and current repair was carried out by 57 local road maintenance units.[7] That were also set up as separate legal entities under MOTC, as well as 2 state enterprises under the Bishkek-Osh State Directorate. In December 2021, a major reform was initiated through Decree #346 of the Cabinet of Ministers "on Measures to Reform the System of the Road Sector." This saw the 4 UADs, the state directorate and its 2 underlying state enterprises, and the 57 DEUs merged into a single state enterprise *Kyrgyzavtozhol*, responsible for implementing all maintenance and current repair works in public roads under annual contracts signed with RMD (these contracts cover all costs of *Kyrgyzavtozhol*). The regional offices remain as separate entities under MOTC and support RMD in the management of the public road network. Other roadworks are contracted out, with *Kyrgyzavtozhol* able to participate in bids.

Road Fund Management

The original Road Fund in the Kyrgyz Republic was created in 1998 through Law #71 "on the Road Fund," with various amendments in later years. However, the Road Fund never became functional, and revenues were never earmarked in practice. In 2018, the Road Fund Law and its amendments were defined invalid through the 2018 Law #55. In 2021 a new Road Fund was established under the MOTC by means of Decree #346 of the Cabinet of Ministers "on Measures to Transform the System of the Road Industry." Subsequently, Law #36 "on the Road Fund" was adopted in April 2022 by the *Jogorku Kenesh* (Parliament) and signed by the President in May 2022. Amendments to the Budget Code related to the Road Fund were introduced in the same month through Law #35 "on making changes to the Budget Code." As per the Road Fund Law, the Road Fund will become operational and receive funding starting January 2023.

---

[4] Департамент Дорожного Хозяйства (ДДХ) / Road Maintenance Department.
[5] Производственно-Линейное Управление Автомобильных Дорог (ПЛУАД) / Production Line Road Administration: Chui, Naryn, Issyk-Kul, and Talas.
[6] Управления Автомобильных Дорог (УАД) / Road Administration: Bishkek-Naryn-Torugart, Osh-Batken-Isfana, Osh-Sarytash-Irkeshtam, and Jalal Abad-Balykchy. These also take care of surrounding roads.
[7] Дорожно-Эксплуатационное Учреждение (ДЭУ) / Road Maintenance Unit.

Eligible Activities

The 2022 Road Fund Law specifies that the Road Fund may be used to finance the activities listed below. This is largely in line with the 1998 law. The Road Fund can also be used to provide subsidies to local governments for the management of public roads within their jurisdictions. The scope of activities that may be funded by the Road Fund is very extensive and puts a high requirement on the available funding of the Road Fund. There are also plans that, from 2025 onward, the funding may also be used to repay interest and principal on loans, putting a further burden on available revenues.

Table 13: Activities Eligible for Financing from the Road Fund

- Design, maintenance, repair, (re)construction, and development of public roads
- Acquisition of machines and equipment for use in public roads
- Development of road and roadside services, and provision of roadside assistance
- Road sector publications by the Ministry of Transport and Communications (standards, manuals, periodicals, etc.)
- Scientific and technical research
- Manage the road industry central and regional bodies within the limits set
- Training and education of staff
- Develop the social environment of the road industry

Source: Law #36 on the Road Fund, 2022.

Management Structure

MOTC was made responsible for the day-to-day operation of the original Road Fund. The 2003 Decree #502 "on the Road Fund Board" identified an 11-member Road Fund Board that was to be chaired by the minister of transport and communications, with other members including representatives of the RMD; *Jogorku Kenesh* (Parliament); Ministry of Finance; Ministry of Local Affairs; State Automobile Inspectorate; Association of Cities; Union of Motorists; Association of Passenger Carriers "*Soyuztrans*"; Association of Road Carriers; and the Planning, Operation, and Construction Department of MOTC. The Road Fund Board was supposed to meet at least twice a year, but in practice never convened.

The new Road Fund secretariat created by the 2021 Decree #346 and subsequent 2022 Law #36 is established as state institute subordinate to MOTC, separate from the RMD that is responsible for managing the implementation of works. The new Road Fund secretariat is headed by a director who is appointed by the Cabinet of Ministers and is responsible for day-to-day operations with support from staff. The director directly appoints and dismisses all other staff of the Road Fund. All decisions are taken by the director, except where these fall under the responsibility of the Supervisory Board. The initial staffing structure of the Road Fund secretariat was approved in the first meeting of the Supervisory Board in January 2022, and includes 20 staff members.

The Supervisory Board is the main decision-making body of the Road Fund. According to Decree #346, the Supervisory Board must consist of a minimum of seven members, with the composition defined by the minister of transport and communications. The first meeting of the Supervisory Board approved the representatives of nine member entities as listed in Table 14.

Table 14: Members of the Road Fund Supervisory Board in the Kyrgyz Republic

- Ministry of Transport and Communications
- Ministry of Finance
- Ministry of Justice
- Ministry of Local Affairs
- Association of Cities
- Union of Motorists
- Association of Passenger Carriers
- Association of Road Carriers
- Association of Engineers

Source: Road Fund secretariat.

Members are appointed for a period of at least 2 years. The Supervisory Board is supposed to meet at least once a month. Decision-making requires a simple majority of votes, with a quorum of five members and at least four members in favor of the decision. The Supervisory Board has the competencies listed in Table 15. The management structure for the Road Fund is presented in Figure 3.

Table 15: Competencies of the Road Fund Supervisory Board in the Kyrgyz Republic

- Defining the tasks of the Road Fund
- Approving the revenue forecasts
- Approving the expenditure plan
- Allocating funds for the design, construction, reconstruction, repair, and maintenance of public roads
- Approving reports
- Approving the amount of funding for the current year and estimated indicators for the following years
- Making proposals to increase revenue levels
- Providing recommendations on the amount of funding for the Road Fund
- Making recommendations on the plan for road repair and maintenance
- Approving the structure, staffing, remuneration levels, employee duties, and rights of the secretariat
- Determining the structure, procedure, and publication of financial statements
- Approving the internal procedures
- Approving the budget for the secretariat
- Controlling the intended use of funds of the Road Fund
- Decision-making regarding international cooperation
- Hearing and approving annual audit reports and Road Fund reports

Source: Decree #346 of the Cabinet of Ministers, 2021.

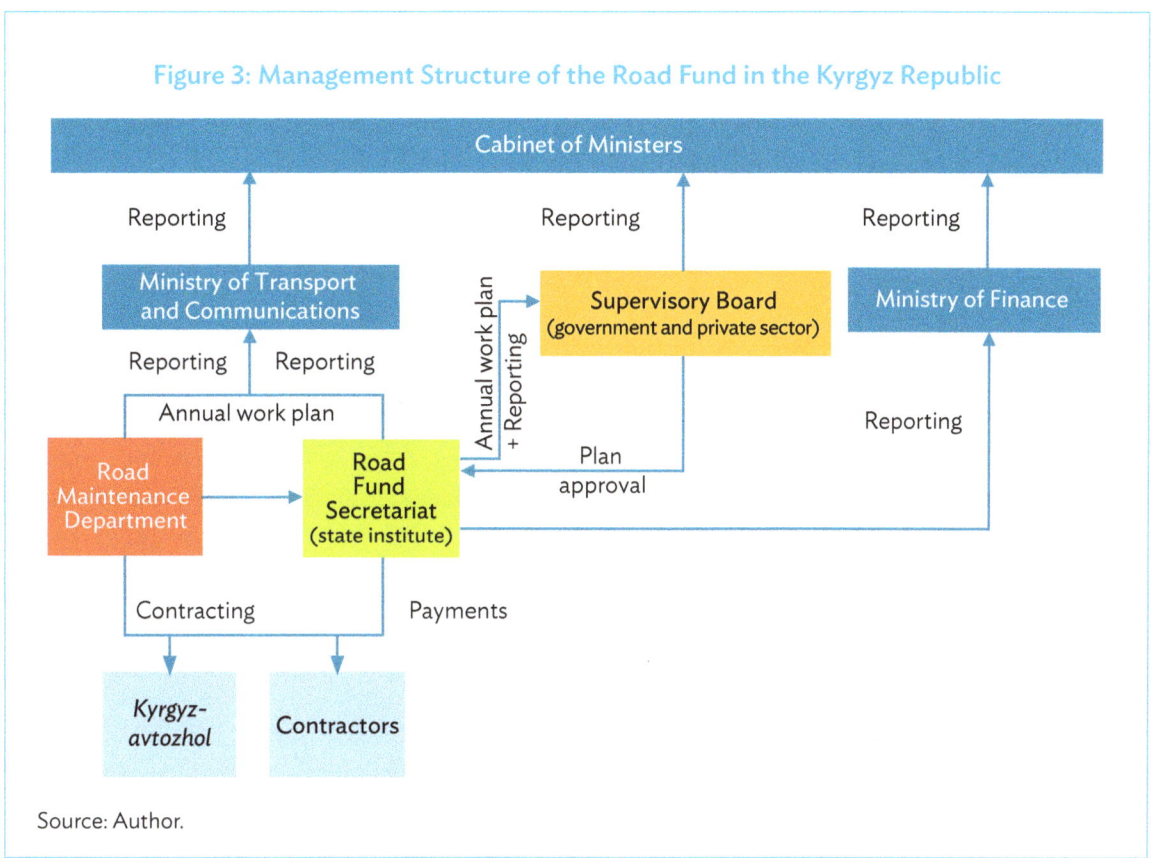

Figure 3: Management Structure of the Road Fund in the Kyrgyz Republic

Source: Author.

Funding Approval and Allocation

The annual work plan is to be prepared by RMD with support from *Kyrgyzavtozhol*. A RAMS was recently developed and a legal framework has been introduced that requires that the RAMS be used in preparing the annual work plan and budget request. The annual work plan will be submitted to the Road Fund secretariat for review and, ultimately, to the Supervisory Board for approval. The Supervisory Board is responsible for ensuring that the annual plan complies with the activities that can be funded by the Road Fund. The Road Fund resolution is not very clear on the procedures for preparing and approving annual work plans, and the procedures for this will need to be defined in more detail in operating procedures for the Road Fund.

The Road Fund regulations are also not very clear on how payments to contractors will be made. According to the Road Fund director and MOTC, the funds will remain in the Road Fund, and RMD will submit certified invoices for payment directly from the Road Fund. This includes payments to *Kyrgyzavtozhol* for implementing road maintenance works, which will be supervised by independent supervision consultants. Responsibility for the proper use of Road Fund financing would then lie with the Road Fund secretariat. The exact approach to be used is best defined in operating procedures for the Road Fund, but these have yet to be prepared and approved by the Supervisory Board.

Financial and Technical Accountability

The 1998 Law "on the Road Fund" required the creation of a special treasury account under the Ministry of Finance, but in practice the special account was never established and earmarked road user charge revenues remained in the Republican Budget, with annual allocations to MOTC and RMD. The new Road Fund created by the 2021 Decree #346 and the 2022 Law #36 is also set up as a separate treasury account under the Ministry of Finance, including a budget account, accumulation account, and a special account. The revenues earmarked for the Road Fund go through the Republican Budget, and are included in the annual budget under a separate budget line for MOTC that is directly transferred to the separate treasury account of the Road Fund. The funds in the special account are targeted and cannot be used for other purposes than indicated in Law #36.

Upon the initial establishment of the Road Fund through Decree #346, any remaining funds at the end of the financial year were to be returned to the Republican Budget as per the Budget Code. However, with the new Law #36 "on the Road Fund" and the corresponding amendments to the Budget Code, unused funds now remain with the Road Fund and can be used in the following year. This greatly facilitates multiannual contracts (e.g., performance-based contracts) and avoids financing problems if works completion is delayed beyond the end of the financial year.

The Road Fund secretariat is required to prepare an annual report regarding revenues and expenditures, indicating expected revenues for the following year. The annual report is to be approved by the Supervisory Board and submitted to the Cabinet of Ministers before the adoption of the new budget for the subsequent year (under the old Road Fund, the annual report was submitted to Parliament). The Road Fund secretariat is required to publish information on the use of the Road Fund financing each year and place this on the MOTC website, although the Road Fund regulations are not clear what information is to be included. Additionally, the Road Fund secretariat is required to submit quarterly financial reports and accounts on budget execution to the Ministry of Finance, in accordance with regulations on accounting and financial reporting in the public sector. Internal audits are to be carried out each year in line with budget legislation.

According to Law #36 "on the Road Fund," the Road Fund is required to carry out audits in accordance with the budget laws. The Road Fund Law does not include any requirement for independent third-party financial audits, although the law allows the Supervisory Board to initiate an independent financial audit. There is no mention of technical audits. There is also no strict requirement to publish the full annual reports or audit reports. The Road Fund regulations leave this to the discretion of the Supervisory Board, which may decide to include these requirements in the standard operating procedures (SOPs) of the Road Fund.

Road Fund Revenue

The abolishment of the Road Fund Law in 2018 did not affect the collection of road user charge revenues, as these were defined in separate laws (Tax Code, Law on Non-Tax Income. and Budget Code, as well as related decrees and resolutions). With the abolishment of the Road Fund Law, these revenues were no longer earmarked for the Road Fund, although in practice the earmarking under the old Road Fund had never been put into practice. Therefore, the revenues from these road user charges continue to form part of the Republican Budget. The establishment of the new Road Fund reintroduced the earmarking of road user charges. The new Road Fund Law and amendments to the Budget Code further strengthen the earmarking of revenues and their transfer to the Road Fund account. The recent establishment of the special treasury accounts and the Road Fund secretariat and Supervisory Board makes it more likely that the annual revenues from these road user charges will actually be transferred to the new Road Fund (a dedicated treasury account was never created for the old road fund, and therefore it could not receive revenues).

Revenue Sources

The revenue sources of the new Road Fund are listed in Table 16. These largely coincide with the revenue sources of the old Road Fund before it was abolished. Originally, the old Road Fund also included revenue from a so-called road tax, which involved a corporate turnover tax paid by businesses. This provided the majority of revenue, but was gradually abolished after 2008, causing a significant decrease in the total revenue of the earmarked road user charges.

Revenue from a vehicle property tax based on vehicle age and engine size was also originally earmarked for the old Road Fund, but it is collected by local governments and was in practice never transferred to the Road Fund, and was eventually removed as an earmarked funding source in 2015.

Table 16: Sources of Funding of the Road Fund (2021)

- Fuel excise tax on gasoline and diesel (at least 50%)
- Vehicle registration fee
- Tolls for passage through artificial structures on public roads
- Tolls from trucks and buses for travel on public roads
- Fees for axle load and size control
- Fees for permits for oversized and/or overweight vehicles with indivisible loads
- Fines for overweight and/or oversized vehicles
- Compensation for damages by heavy and oversized vehicles
- Fees for lease of land in the right-of-way of public roads
- Payments related to public–private partnerships
- Republican Budget allocations for design, (re)construction, repair, and maintenance of public roads and structures
- Foreign investments and grants
- Non refundable funds received from individuals and legal entities, including voluntary donations
- Proceeds from the collection of fees for licenses and permits for road and water transport

Source: Law #36 on the Road Fund, 2022.

The new Road Fund introduces two new earmarked revenues in the form of fines for overweight and/or oversized vehicles (in addition to fees) and payments from public–private partnership (PPP) agreements. Apart from the revenue related to road user charges, both the old and the new road funds can also receive allocations from the Republican Budget and from foreign investments and grants. The customs duty on imported vehicles is not earmarked for the Road Fund, despite providing significant revenue that is allocated to the Republican Budget. A few other fees are directly related to road use, but are not earmarked for the Road Fund, including permit fees for international vehicles and permit fees for passenger and goods transporters that are collected directly by RMD. The government is considering the earmarking of additional road user charges with the aim of increasing the revenue of the Road Fund. Expected revenues and expenditures are to be included in the annual law on the Republican Budget under a separate budget line.

Fuel excise tax. The fuel excise tax is the most important source of revenue for the new Road Fund and is applied to gasoline and diesel (although excise tax is collected on natural gas, this is not earmarked for the Road Fund). The excise tax rates are defined in the Tax Code, and any changes require a change to the Tax Code. The fuel excise tax for fuel imported from countries outside the Eurasian Economic Union is collected by the State Customs Service, while for fuel imported from inside the Eurasian Economic Union (which is imported duty-free) and for fuel produced domestically, the excise tax is collected by the State Tax Service. Of the collected fuel excise tax revenue, at least 50% is earmarked for the Road Fund. This percentage appears to have been originally set in the old Road Fund based on the percentage of fuel used by road users. The current percentage of fuel consumption attributable to road users may be higher and could warrant an increase of this percentage. The percentage may be increased through an amendment of the Road Fund regulations by the Cabinet of Ministers. The excise tax rates for gasoline and diesel defined in the 2022 Tax Code are presented in Table 17. These are the tax rates introduced in August 2020, providing a doubling compared to previous rates of Som5,000 per ton for gasoline and Som800 per ton for diesel.

Table 17: Fuel Excise Tax Rates

Fuel type	Rate (Som/ton)	Rate (US$/ton)	Rate (US$/liter)
Gasoline	Som10,000/ton	$103/ton	$0.087/liter
Diesel	Som2,000/ton	$21/ton	$0.021/liter

Source: Tax Code, 2022.

Vehicle registration fee. The vehicle registration fee is regulated by the Code on Non-Tax Incomes and the rules for registration and reregistration of vehicles issued through Resolution #407 of 2017. Collection of the vehicle registration fee is carried out by the Department for the Registration of Vehicles and Drivers under the State Registration Service. The vehicle registration fee is charged when a vehicle is imported into the country (first registration) and whenever there is a change in ownership (reregistration). First registration of a vehicle involves a fee of 5% of the tax value of the vehicle, while for the reregistration this drops to 0.3% of the tax value. The tax value is determined by the engine capacity and age of the vehicle, as well as the country where the vehicle was manufactured (the tax value for vehicles from member countries of the Eurasian Economic Union is generally lower, especially in the case of newer vehicles). The tax value drops with increasing age of the vehicle until it reaches 10 years of age. Table 18 shows the initial registration and reregistration fees for new vehicles (maximum rates) and for vehicles of 10 years or older (minimum rates). Initial registration fees range from $70 to $2,160 for cars and $125–$2,560 for trucks and buses. Electric vehicles are exempt from paying the registration fee, while hybrid vehicles pay only 50% of the fee. In 2017 a total of 137,691 vehicles were registered, of which 29,264 were imported vehicles (first registrations).

Table 18: Vehicle Registration and Reregistration Fees
(Som)

Vehicle Type	Engine Capacity	Initial Registration Fee (5%)				Reregistration Fee (0.3%)			
		New Vehicle		>10 Years Old		New Vehicle		>10 Years Old	
		Inside EAEU	Outside EAEU	Inside EAEU	Outside EAEU	Inside EAEU	Outside EAEU	Inside EAEU	Outside EAEU
Cars	<1,000 cc	17,500	37,375	2,500	4,000	1,050	2,243	150	240
	1,000–2,000 cc	19,000	48,875	3,500	5,000	1,140	2,933	210	300
	2,000–3,000 cc	20,500	57,500	4,500	6,000	1,230	3,450	270	360
	3,000–4,000 cc	22,000	66,125	5,500	7,000	1,320	3,968	330	420
	4,000–5,000 cc	23,500	71,875	6,500	8,000	1,410	4,313	390	480
	>5,000 cc	25,000	77,625	7,500	10,000	1,500	4,658	450	600
Buses, minibuses, trucks	<2,000 cc	33,000	55,200	4,500	8,000	1,980	3,312	270	480
	2,000–3,000 cc	35,000	63,250	5,000	9,500	2,100	3,795	300	570
	3,000–4,000 cc	39,000	71,300	5,500	11,000	2,340	4,278	330	660
	3,000–5,000 cc	39,000	74,750	5,500	11,750	2,340	4,485	330	705
	5,000–8,000 cc	42,500	79,350	5,750	12,500	2,550	4,761	345	750
	8,000–10,000 cc	46,000	87,400	6,250	14,000	2,760	5,244	375	840
	10,000–12,000 cc	55,000	89,125	6,750	15,000	3,300	5,348	405	900
	12,000–15,000 cc	57,500	90,275	6,850	16,000	3,450	5,417	411	960
	>15,000 cc	60,000	92,000	7,000	17,500	3,600	5,520	420	1,050
Motorcycles	<350 cc	7,500		2,250		450		135	
	>350 cc	22,500		5,000		1,350		300	

cc = cubic centimeter, EAEU = Eurasian Economic Union.
Source: State Registration Service.

Tolls for passage through artificial structures in public roads. Tolling for passage through artificial structures is regulated in the Code on Non-Tax Income. Tolls are collected from all vehicles using artificial structures (e.g., tunnels). Currently, tolls are collected only at the two major tunnels along the Bishkek–Osh road (Sosnovka and Karakol tunnels). Collection is carried out by the State Directorate Bishkek-Osh, which has been merged recently into the state enterprise *Kyrgyzavtozhol*. Although revenue was earmarked formally to the Road Fund, in practice it remained with the State Directorate and was used for the maintenance and repair of the Bishkek–Osh road, especially its tunnels.

Tolls for travel on public roads. Tolling on public roads is regulated in the Code on Non-Tax Income and the 2008 Decree #615 "on Toll Roads." Currently there are no tolls collected on public roads, but MOTC is planning to introduce tolls in 4,400 km of public roads in the form of fees for trucks and buses that use those roads. The tolling will make use of an automated registration system that will include a dimension scanner and dynamic scales to measure axle and total loads. The toll rate would gradually increase to Som8.3/km ($0.86). According to the decree on toll roads, toll collection is the responsibility of RMD. The decree also requires that an alternative route must exist for any toll road, with the length of the alternative route at most being 3 times as long.

Oversized and overweight vehicle fees and fines. The remaining revenue sources include fees and fines regarding axle load and dimension control, permits for oversized and overweight vehicles with indivisible loads, fines for oversized and overweight vehicles, and compensation for damages caused by heavy vehicles. These fees are regulated by the Code on Non-Tax Income and by the 2011 Resolution #454 providing the procedures for these fees. The revenue from these sources is collected by the Department of Automobile, Water Transport and Weight and Dimension Control under MOTC, except for the fines for overloaded and/or oversized vehicles that are collected by the traffic police.

Revenue Levels

Although the old Road Fund Law earmarked revenues from different road user charges, the Road Fund never functioned in practice. Instead of earmarked revenues being transferred to the Road Fund, the government made annual allocations from the Republican Budget to MOTC that were, more or less, in line with the expected Road Fund revenues. Actual budget allocations were largely in line with earmarked revenues up until 2009. In 2009, the road tax was gradually abolished, with revenues from this tax dropping from Som963 million in 2008 to only Som138 million in 2009 and Som48 million in 2010. Republican Budget allocations continued, more or less, at the same level; however, significantly exceeding the revenues of earmarked road user charges.

Table 19: Earmarked Road User Charge Revenues 2008–2012
(Som million)

Earmarked Revenue Source	2008		2009		2010		2011		2012	
Road tax	962.9	69%	138.4	19%	48.4	5%	3.6	0%	4.2	0%
Fuel excise tax	209.5	15%	275.5	37%	259.6	29%	346.9	45%	439.4	41%
Vehicle registration fee	190.9	14%	279.7	38%	565.2	62%	345.5	45%	546.4	51%
Fee for load and dimension control	0.0	0%	0.0	0%	0.0	0%	18.0	2%	29.5	3%
Tolls (tunnels)	41.4	3%	51.4	7%	35.0	4%	49.9	7%	50.7	5%
Total	1,404.7	100%	745.1	100%	908.2	100%	763.9	100%	1,070.1	100%
Allocated budget	1,564.5	111%	1,655.1	222%	1,552.5	171%	1,342.2	176%	1,633.8	153%

Source: European Bank for Reconstruction and Development Road User Study Charges Report, 2014.

Since 2008, however, Republican Budget allocations have only increased marginally in som terms and have actually reduced in US dollar terms. In this same period, revenues from vehicle registration fees and especially the fuel excise tax have continued to increase, and Republican Budget allocations now fall way below the revenue levels of the earmarked road user charges. In addition, the years 2020 and 2021 saw significant reductions in allocated budgets as a result of the COVID-19 pandemic.

Table 20: Republican Budget Allocations to Road Maintenance and Repair

Year	Som Million	US$ Million
2010	1,552.5	$33.7
2011	1,342.2	$29.0
2012	1,633.8	$34.7
2013	2,021.3	$41.7
2014	2,150.7	$40.0
2015	1,892.7	$29.9
2016	1,866.3	$24.7
2017	1,979.8	$26.2
2018	1,984.0	$28.5
2019	1,963.3	$28.1
2020	720.8	$9.5
2021	1,558.1	$18.4

Source: Ministry of Transport and Communications.

In 2018, revenues from the earmarked road user charges already surpassed the allocated budgets. The reported revenue from the fuel excise tax in 2018 was Som3.6 billion ($52 million), mostly from gasoline consumption. With 50% of the revenue earmarked for the road fund, this forms the main revenue source at Som1.8 billion ($26 million). Vehicle registration fees generated a revenue of Som0.5 billion in 2018, while other earmarked fees generated a further Som0.2 billion as shown in Table 21. Altogether, the earmarked road user charges generated $36 million in revenues in 2018, 25% more than the allocated budget for road maintenance and repair for that year.

It must be noted, however, that in 2020 the fuel excise tax rates were doubled, resulting in significantly higher revenues (the impact in 2020 and 2021 was limited to a certain degree because of a decrease in consumption because of COVID-19). Current gasoline consumption is reported to be in the order of 485,000 tons per year and for diesel consumption it is in the order of 475,000 tons per year. As a result, the current fuel excise tax revenue is expected to be in the order of Som5.8 billion, 60% higher than in 2018. The earmarked allocation to the road fund would then amount to Som2.9 billion ($36 million). Total revenue of the Road Fund when it starts operation in 2023 is expected to be in the order of Som4 billion ($50 million). This excludes tolls for trucks and buses travelling on public roads that have yet to be introduced, and that are expected by MOTC to gradually provide about Som3.5 billion in additional annual revenues over time.

Table 21: Earmarked Revenues in 2018

Revenue Source	Som Million	US$ Million
Fuel excise tax (50%)	1,784.5	$26.2
Vehicle registration fee	485.6	$7.1
Fee for load and dimension control	77.6	$1.1
Permit fee for vehicles with indivisible loads	15.3	$0.2
Fee for compensation of damages	20.9	$0.3
Tolls for tunnels	59.4	$0.9
Total	**2,443.3**	**$35.8**

Source: Ministry of Transport and Communications.

Revenue Allocation

The budget allocations to the different activities are presented in Table 22. This includes the allocations to management and administration by the central office of RMD, as well as the allocations to rehabilitation of international road corridors (this primarily involves development partner funding complemented by government counterpart funding).

Table 22: National Budget Allocations to Roads
(Som million)

Budget Line	2018 Actual	2019 Actual	2020 Actual	2021 Preliminary	2022 Budgeted
Management and administration	40	43	35	43	88
Maintenance and repair of public roads	1,953	1,940	787	690	2,154
Design and survey work	18	7	7	0	1
Capital repairs	54	29	3	0	20
Midterm repair	1,117	940	217	120	1,439
Current repair	365	497	224	227	300
Winter and summer maintenance	204	267	213	198	198
Road signage	11	13	0.3	0	0
Administration costs	184	187	123	145	196
Rehabilitation of international roads	6,104	8,412	5,984	8,045	10,141
Total	**8,097**	**10,394**	**6,806**	**8,778**	**12,383**
Exchange rate	68.2	69.5	75.8	84.7	84.8
Total US$ million	**$118.8**	**$149.6**	**$89.6**	**$103.7**	**$146.1**

Source: Budget 2020, Budget 2022.

The influence of COVID-19 is clearly visible in 2020 and 2021 with a reduction in the budget allocated to maintenance and repair, from $28 million to $29 million in previous years to $10 million in 2020 and $8 million in 2021. Funding for these years came from the general budget, with allocations transferred to other sectors in response to the decreased revenues and pandemic response. As such, the decrease in funding for road maintenance and repair has been much more severe than in countries with road funds and earmarked revenues. In the Kyrgyz Republic, allocations to winter and summer maintenance and administration costs were cut by 25%–40%, while allocations to current repair were cut by 60%. Allocations to midterm repair were cut by as much as 80%–90%, causing a severe maintenance backlog. Although the 2022 budget foresees significant allocations to midterm repairs, it has yet to be seen if this can be achieved in practice. Allocations to current repair continue to be lower than before the pandemic.

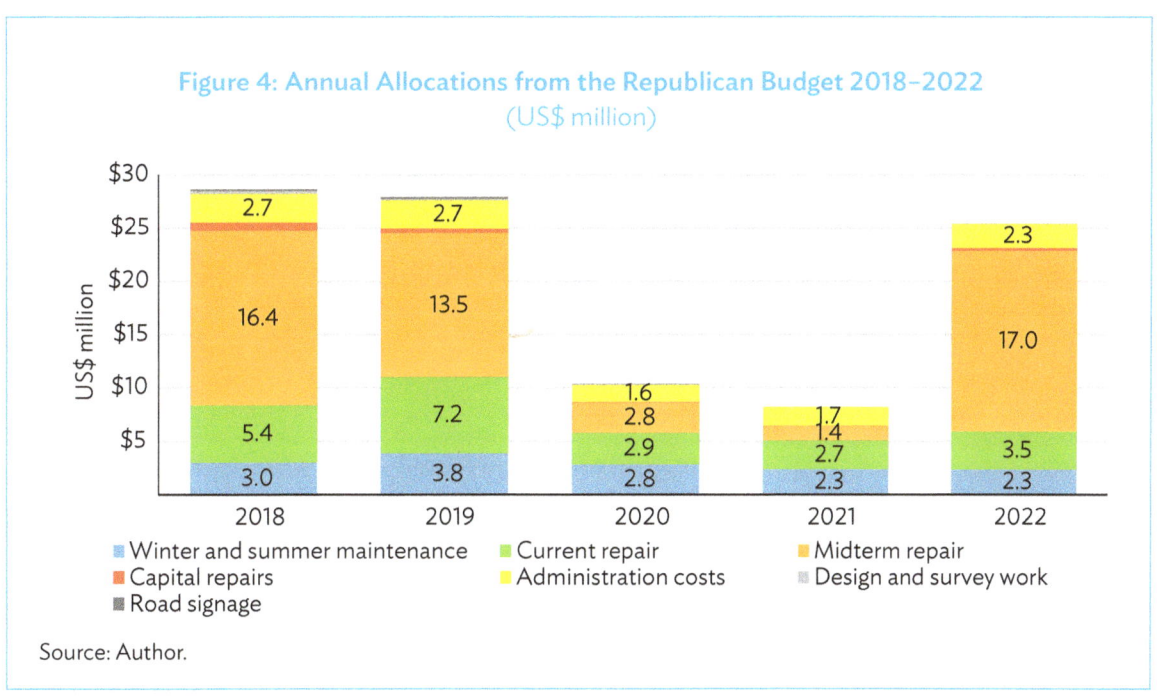

Figure 4: Annual Allocations from the Republican Budget 2018–2022 (US$ million)

Source: Author.

Funding Needs

An HDM4 strategy analysis carried out in 2021 by Asian Development Bank (ADB) consultants based on recently collected data for the public road network identified an optimum 20-year funding need for road maintenance and repair of $120 million per year. This does not include an additional requirement of $1,040 million to address the maintenance and repair backlog. The long-term maintenance and repair needs would include about $80 million per year for the 8,100 km of paved roads and $40 million per year for the 10,700 km of unpaved roads (some unpaved roads would receive only maintenance and current repair). In terms of administrative road classes, it would include about $45 million for the 4,219 km of international roads, $30 million for the 5,616 km of national roads, and $45 million for the 9,107 km of local roads. About half the long-term maintenance and repair budget would need to be allocated to midterm repair (this does not take account of the additional capital repair needs related to the maintenance and repair backlog).

MOTC estimates its maintenance and repair needs at Som10.6 billion per year ($125 million), which is largely in line with the HDM4 analysis. They estimate that a larger portion is required for international roads (about half, Som5.7 billion). The costs for maintenance, current repair, and midterm repair amount to Som7.1 billion ($85 million). These cost estimates are calculated based on the length of roads divided by the frequency with which treatments need to be repeated, and multiplied by the unit cost of the treatment concerned. This assumes that routine maintenance and current repair are carried out every year and in all roads (18,810 km) at an annual cost of Som2.4 billion ($28 million). Midterm repair includes regravelling of gravel roads every 4 years, resurfacing of black gravel roads (gravel mixed with bitumen) every 6 years, new surface treatments every 5 years, and overlays for asphalt concrete roads every 10 years. Rehabilitation of the asphalt concrete roads is planned every 15 years.

Table 23: Calculation of Maintenance and Repair Needs by the Ministry of Transport and Communications

Treatment Type	Frequency	Length per Year	Unit Cost (Som/km)	Total (Som '000)	Total (US$ million)
Maintenance (5%)	every year	-	-	550,000	$6.5
Routine repair	every year	18,810 km	14,000–191,000	1,850,000	$21.9
Midterm repair				4,210,000	$49.7
Surface treatment	5 years	600 km	1,000,000	600,000	$7.1
Overlay	10 years	400 km	5,000,000	2,000,000	$23.6
Black gravel course	6 years	280 km	2,500,000	700,000	$8.3
Regravelling	4 years	2,270 km	400,000	910,000	$10.7
Capital repair (asphalt concrete)	15 years	320 km	11,000,000	3,520,000	$41.6
Engineering structures				500,000	$5.9
Total				10,630,000	$125.6

- = not available, km = kilometer.
Source: Ministry of Transport and Communications.

Pre–COVID-19 budget allocations to maintenance and repair were in the order of $28 million per year, about 20%–25% of the identified needs. For the new Road Fund, revenues are expected to be in the order of Som4 billion (about $50 million). This is a significant increase from the pre–COVID-19 allocations from the Republican Budget, but remains far below the identified funding needs for road maintenance and repair that are in the order of Som10 billion ($125 million). Budget allocation to other activities eligible for financing from the Road Fund would further increase the funding needs.

Over time, additional revenues are expected from the introduction of tolls for trucks and buses on public roads. MOTC estimates that these would generate a further Som3.5 billion (over $40 million) per year in revenue. This would allow the maintenance and repair needs for international and national roads to be covered. However, it is far from certain that this toll revenue will actually be achieved, and it will take several years before the toll revenue will be generated.

MONGOLIA

Mongolia has 15,249 km of international and state roads, nearly half of which are unpaved, primarily earthen tracks. The international and state roads are managed by the Ministry of Roads and Transport Development (MRTD), through the state-owned enterprise Road and Transport Development Center (RTDC). Maintenance as well as routine, regular, and emergency repairs are managed through the RTDC's Road Maintenance Department, with implementation carried out by the 20 state road maintenance companies (AZZAs) under RTDC. Major repair and (re)construction are contracted out to licensed legal entities from the private sector through competitive bidding and supervised by independent consultants.

Road Fund Management

The State Road Fund was originally created under the 1998 Law on Roads, together with local road funds at capital city and *aimag* (province) level. In 2017 a new Law on Roads was issued, which continues with this division. The State Road Fund is set up as a special fund under the Law on Special Funds, which expressly mentions the State Road Fund as one of the special funds. The 2019 Decree #312 issues the regulations for the State Road Fund and defines the revenue allocation to the State Road Fund from the gasoline and diesel tax.

Eligible Activities

The 1998 Law on Roads defined that the State Road Fund would finance the construction, repair, and maintenance of international and national roads and related facilities, as well as equipment procurement for the AZZAs and road inspections. The 2017 Law on Roads, however, limits the scope of the new State Road Fund to financing maintenance (excluding pavement and structure repairs), routine repair (of pavements and structures), regular repair (periodic maintenance), major repair (rehabilitation), and emergency repairs of international and state roads. The 2019 regulations define that at least 90% of funding is to be used for maintenance and repair of international and state roads, giving priority to maintenance, routine repair, and emergency repairs. The Law on Roads and the regulations also allow up to 10% of funds to be used for equipment procurement for the maintenance units and for carrying out inspections and staff training. Although not explicitly mentioned in the Law on Roads, the 2019 regulations define that funding may also be used for road safety measures and improvements, although it is not clear whether this falls under the 90% or the 10% portion of the available funding. The Law on Roads prohibits the use of State Road Fund financing for other purposes.

Table 24: Activities Eligible for Financing from the State Road Fund

- Summer and winter maintenance
- Routine repairs
- Regular repairs
- Emergency repairs
- Capital repairs
- Safety improvements
- Equipment procurement
- Inspections
- Staff training

Sources: 2017 Law on Roads, and 2019 Road Fund Regulations.

Management Structure

The responsibility for the administration of the State Road Fund is allocated to RTDC under MRTD as the central administrative body in charge of roads. The State Road Fund is set up under RTDC, falling under its Toll Collection, Road Use and Traffic Control Department. According to the 2019 regulations for the State Road Fund, RTDC is responsible for preparing the annual plan for the use of the expected State Road Fund financing and submitting this to the Ministry of Finance for approval. The approved plan is reflected in the annual Budget Law. The 2017 audit of the State Road Fund recommended that the State Road Fund be set up as a legal entity, separate from RTDC, but this has not happened.

The Law on Government Special Funds requires that nongovernment organizations and professional associations be included in the monitoring of the special fund. The 2017 Law on Roads introduces a Road Board consisting of representatives of road users and citizens, which is responsible for exercising public control over the revenues, expenditure, road conditions, and road safety. The 2019 Decree #312 mentions that the public control over the revenue and expenditure of the State Road Fund will be exercised by the Road Board, consisting of representatives of road users and citizens. This Road Board has a monitoring role, and does not appear to be involved in decision-making or in the approval of the annual work plan. The management structure of the State Road Fund is presented in Figure 5.

Funding Approval and Allocation

The work plan is prepared by RTDC and submitted to the State Road Fund for approval. However, the secretariat of the State Road Fund is a subordinate division of RTDC. The Road Board is only involved in monitoring of the State Road Fund and is not involved in the approval of the annual work plan. This means that the State Road Fund approval process is largely an internal MRTD and/or RTDC process with no inputs from other ministries or entities. The only external approval process is by the Ministry of Finance, to which RTDC has to submit the annual work plan for approval before the State Road Fund can proceed with financing the planned works.

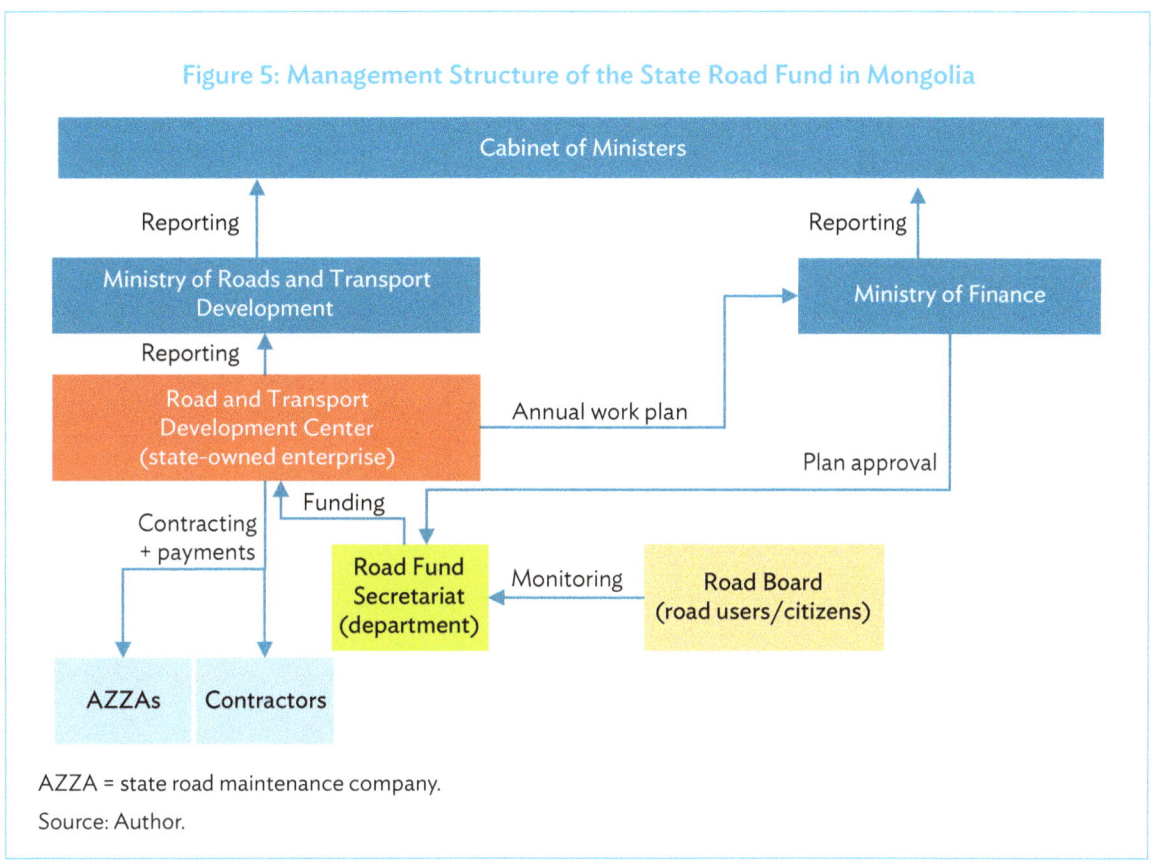

Figure 5: Management Structure of the State Road Fund in Mongolia

AZZA = state road maintenance company.
Source: Author.

Once the work plan is approved, the funding is transferred from the State Road Fund to MRTD and RTDC. The State Road Fund is not involved in the actual use of the funding, and does not check invoices or make payments. This is all managed by RTDC, and the State Road Fund basically has a similar function to the General Budget of transferring an agreed funding amount to the budget entity, in this case MRTD.

Financial and Technical Accountability

Under the Law on Government Special Funds, the State Road Fund is set up as a special budget account under the Ministry of Finance as part of the state budget. The State Road Fund is listed as one of the special funds in Mongolia, although no further description is provided in the law as is the case for the other special funds.

The Law on Government Special Funds requires that semiannual and annual reports are submitted to the Ministry of Finance. The law further requires that the annual report be audited in accordance with the Law on State Audit. This audit is carried out by the State Audit Office and may include financial, performance, and compliance auditing. Financial audit reports were initially prepared by the State Audit Office every 2 years, covering 2 financial years. In recent years, the financial audit reports have been prepared annually. Independent financial audits are reported to be carried out each year by private companies, forming the basis for the financial audit report of the State Audit Office.

The Law on Government Special Funds requires that the annual report and audit results as well as general information on expenditure, execution, financed projects, and activities are reported on the website of the fund, as well as through the national transparency website Glass Account. The State Road Fund currently does not have a website, and only limited information is provided on the RTDC website. The financial audit reports have repeatedly recorded it as an issue that the State Road Fund is not included in the Glass Account since it is not an independent legal entity. The financial audit reports are made available on the State Audit Office website, but are not structurally published on the MRTD website.

Road Fund Revenue

The 2017 Law on Roads identifies road user charges of which the revenues are earmarked for the new State Road Fund. However, in practice these were not fully allocated to the State Road Fund, limiting available revenues and the volume of road maintenance and repair that could be carried out. Up to 2020 the revenue of the State Road Fund was limited to toll revenue collected directly by RTDC. In 2020 the allocation to the State Road Fund increased significantly, with allocations better complying with earmarked revenues, although revenues from smaller road user charges are still not allocated to the State Road Fund.

Revenue Sources

The 2017 Law on Roads identifies the sources of revenue of the State Road Fund as listed in Table 25. The Law on Roads does not mention the tax on gasoline and diesel fuel, which was included in the 1998 version of the law. However, this revenue source is earmarked for the State Road Fund through the 1995 Law "on Gasoline and Diesel Tax" and, subsequently, was included in the 2019 regulations for the State Road Fund. The tax on motor vehicles included in the 1998 Law on Roads is no longer included as a revenue source since collection is done at the local level, making this less suitable for financing the central State Road Fund (this road user charge continues to fund the local road funds).[8]

Table 25: Sources of Funding of the State Road Fund

- At least 20% of vehicle excise tax
- Tax on gasoline and diesel
- Fees for the use of international, national, and special-purpose roads (tolls)
- International vehicle fees
- Traffic fines issued on international, national, and special-purpose roads
- Fees for the use of the right-of-way in international, national, and special-purpose roads
- State budget allocations
- Foreign loans, grants, and donations

Sources: Law on Roads, 2017 and Law on Gasoline and Diesel Tax, 1995.

---

[8] Sources of funding for the local road funds include the vehicle tax, traffic fines issued in local roads, parking fees, fees for the use of the right-of-way of local roads, local budget allocations, and loans and grants for local roads.

Vehicle excise tax. The excise tax on imported vehicles is regulated by the 2006 Law on Special Excise Tax and subsequent amendments. The rate of excise tax depends on the age of the vehicle and on the engine capacity as shown in Table 26 for gasoline- and diesel-powered vehicles. Interesting is the fact that vehicle excise tax rates increase for older vehicles, ranging from $286 to $5,424 for new gasoline- or diesel-powered vehicles to $3,817–$25,181 for vehicles over 10 years old. For vehicles powered by natural gas that make up about 70% of vehicle imports, the rates are 50% of those shown in Table 26. For electric vehicles the excise rates are 50% of the rates shown for gasoline- and diesel-powered engines of less than 1,500 cc. The increasing tax rates for older vehicles and the reduced rates for natural gas and electrical vehicles motivate the import of newer vehicles with lower emissions. The tax is collected by the Mongolian Customs General Administration upon entry of the vehicle into the country. Of the total revenue collected, 20% is earmarked currently for the State Road Fund (this is in line with the minimum percentage set in the Law on Roads).

Table 26: Vehicle Excise Tax
(MNT)

Engine Capacity	<3 Years Old	4–6 Years Old	7–9 Years Old	>10 Years Old
<1,500 cc	750,000	1,600,000	3,350,000	10,000,000
1,500–2,500 cc	2,300,000	3,200,000	5,000,000	11,700,000
2,500–3,500 cc	3,050,000	4,000,000	6,700,000	13,350,000
3,500–4,500 cc	6,850,750	8,000,000	10,850,000	17,500,000
>4,500 cc	14,210,000	27,200,000	39,150,000	65,975,000

cc = cubic centimeter.
Source: 2006 Law on Special Excise Tax.

Tax on gasoline and diesel. This tax is regulated by the 1995 Law on Gasoline and Diesel Tax. This law defines the tax rates, complicating amendments to the rates to correct for inflation and respond to funding needs, which would require a change to the law and cannot be achieved by a decree or other legal instrument. As a result, the rates have remained unchanged since 1995. Where the rates were originally equivalent to about 4.1 US dollar cents per liter for gasoline and 0.5 US dollar cents per liter for diesel, because of the devaluation of the togrog, the revenue has now dropped to 0.6 US dollar cents per liter for gasoline and less than 0.1 US dollar cents per liter for diesel. These rates are extremely low compared to other countries, especially for diesel where the rate was low to start with.

An additional issue is that the 2017 Law on Roads does not specifically earmark this tax to the State Road Fund and, as a result, the revenue was not being received by the fund. The 2019 Decree #312 corrects this situation, linking up to the Law on Gasoline and Diesel Tax that earmarks the revenue from this tax to the State Road Fund. Decree #312 defines a percentage of the revenue to be allocated to the State Road Fund, increasing gradually from 70% of gasoline and 84% of diesel tax revenue in 2020 to 96% of gasoline and 93% of diesel tax revenue from 2023 onward. It is unclear why the percentages do not increase to 100%, but this appears to be in order to offset the collection costs (only net revenues are transferred).

This tax on gasoline and diesel is different from the excise tax on fuel that is regulated by the 2006 Law on Special Excise Tax, with rates of MNT15,950/MNT21,750 per ton for gasoline (about 0.5 US dollar cents per liter) and MNT21,750 per ton for diesel (0.7 US dollar cents per liter). Although the excise tax rates on gasoline are slightly lower than the tax rates on gasoline earmarked for the Sate Road Fund, the rate of the diesel excise tax is 10 times higher than the diesel tax earmarked for the State Road Fund, resulting in significantly higher revenues. However, the revenue from the fuel excise tax is not earmarked for the State Road Fund and remains in the state budget.

Table 27: Tax on Gasoline and Diesel

Fuel Type	Tax Rate (MNT/ton)	Allocation to Road Fund (MNT/ton)	Tax Rate (US$/liter)	Allocation to Road Fund (US$/liter)
Gasoline up to 90 octane	MNT20,350	MNT20,000	$0.0057	$0.0056
Gasoline over 90 octane	MNT25,700		$0.0072	
Diesel	MNT2,140	MNT2,000	$0.0007	$0.0007

Sources: 1995 Law on Gasoline and Diesel Tax, and 2019 Decree #312.

Tolls. Tolling is regulated by the Law on Roads, which provides the Ministry of Transport and Roads with the authority to define the procedures for tolling in international, national, and special purpose roads. The 2016 Government Resolution #103 defines the toll rates to be applied in international, national, and special purpose roads as presented in Table 28. For the highway to the airport, specific toll rates are defined in Government Resolution #282 of 2019, also presented in Table 28. The tolling procedures are defined in the 2021 Ministerial Decree #106. Collection of the tolls in international, national, and special purpose roads is carried out by RTDC through its Toll Collection, Road Use, and Traffic Control Department (the same department that manages the State Road Fund). Toll collection costs were high, averaging over 30% in 2014–2015, and exceeding 60% in nearly half the toll stations in those years. The high toll collection costs are being addressed through the introduction of an electronic toll collection system using smart cards. However, because of the low traffic volumes on many roads in Mongolia, toll collection costs will continue to form a significant portion of the toll revenue.

Table 28: Toll Rates

Vehicle Type	General			Ulaanbaatar-Khushig Valley Airport		
	Category	Rate (MNT)	Rate (US$)	Category	Rate (MNT)	Rate (US$)
Passenger vehicles	<12 seats	MNT1,000	$0.38	<8 seats	MNT2,000	$0.76
	12–24 seats	MNT2,000	$0.76	8-16 seats	MNT10,000	$3.82
	>24 seats	MNT3,000	$1.15	>16 seats	MNT20,000	$7.63

continued on next page

Table 28 continued

Vehicle Type	General			Ulaanbaatar-Khushig Valley Airport		
	Category	Rate (MNT)	Rate (US$)	Category	Rate (MNT)	Rate (US$)
Freight vehicles	<3.5 tons, 2 axles	MNT2,000	$0.76	<3.5 tons	MNT5,000	$1.91
	3.5-18 tons, 2 axles	MNT3,000	$1.15	3.5-7.5 tons	MNT10,000	$3.82
	<18 tons, 3 axles	MNT4,000	$1.53	<7.5 tons	MNT15,000	$5.73
	18-25 tons, 3 axles	MNT5,000	$1.91	Truck+Trailer	MNT20,000	$7.63
	<25 tons, 4 axles	MNT6,000	$2.29			
	>25 tons, 4 axles	MNT10,000	$3.82			
Others	Equipment	MNT10,000	$3.82			
	Motorcycle	MNT500	$0.19	Motorcycle	MNT2,000	$0.76

Sources: 2016 Government Resolution #103, and 2019 Government Resolution #282.

Other fees and fines. The Law on Roads also earmarks the revenues of other fees and fines to the State Road Fund. This includes fees for foreign vehicles to make use of the road network; traffic fines issued on international, national, and special purpose roads; and fees for the use of the right-of-way. Revenues from these road user charges are less significant, and in practice are not being allocated to the State Road Fund.

Revenue Levels

For considerable time, the revenue levels of the State Road Fund have been very low. Until 2020, the revenue was limited to the toll revenue collected directly by RTDC. This toll revenue has been steadily increasing with ever-growing traffic levels and a gradual increase in the number of toll stations, from 11 in 2014 to 24 in 2020. As a result, toll revenues in US dollar terms doubled from $1.5 million in 2014 to $3.3 million in 2020 (in togrog terms they tripled). However, toll collection costs were high, with toll operating costs of the State Road Fund forming 33% of collected toll revenue in 2016 and continuing to form 35% of collected toll revenue in 2020. Although the operating costs cover more than only toll collection costs, over three-quarters of the operating costs are formed by staff salaries and pensions, with the majority of staff involved in toll collection. Especially for the toll stations in roads with low traffic volumes, the collection costs have been high, often exceeding 60% of collected revenue and, in some cases, even exceeding 100% of collected revenue (toll collection actually cost more than it provided in revenue). Although the collection costs as a percentage of collected revenue continue to decrease, this does limit the potential for further expansion of the number of toll stations.

Revenues from the gasoline and diesel tax increased by 50% in togrog terms between 2014 and 2020, but remained steady in US dollar terms, increasing only slightly from $6.3 million in 2014 to $6.5 million in 2020. Although increased consumption resulted in increased revenues, the fixed rates from 1995 meant that revenues were not able to match inflation and the devaluation of the togrog. This revenue was not transferred to the State Road Fund however, especially after the new Law on Roads failed to earmark it as a revenue source. However, the 2019 Decree #312 allocated most of the gasoline and diesel tax revenue to the State Road Fund and, since 2020, this revenue appears to be transferred to the State Road Fund (in the financial audit report, it is presented as income from the state budget). As mentioned earlier, this tax is different from the fuel excise tax that has significantly higher revenue levels ($96.5 million in 2020), but is not earmarked for the State Road Fund.

Similarly, the 20% of the vehicle excise tax that was earmarked for the State Road Fund was also not being transferred to the State Road Fund for many years. Revenue levels from the vehicle excise tax doubled in togrog terms between 2014 and 2020, increasing by 33% in US dollar terms from $49 million in 2014 to $66 million in 2020. However, only 20% of these revenues are earmarked for the State Road Fund, equivalent to $13 million in 2020. This is the minimum percentage set in the Law on Roads, and could potentially be increased to provide more revenue to the State Road Fund.

In 2020, the revenue levels of the State Road Fund jumped from $3.4 million in 2019 (toll revenue only) to $20.8 million in 2020. In addition to the $3.3 million in toll revenue, $17.5 million was transferred from the state budget, understood to be a combination of the gasoline and diesel tax revenues and the vehicle excise tax revenues. The revenues in togrog are presented in Table 29, while Figure 6 shows the revenue in US dollar terms.

Table 29: Annual Revenues of the State Road Fund 2014–2020
(MNT million)

Source	2014	2015	2016	2017	2018	2019	2020
Toll collection	2,901	3,058	4,970	7,007	7,678	8,866	8,648
Donations	-	-	-	-	60	25	-
Other income	-	-	10	14	6	10	9
Balance from previous year	1,593	1,939	-	-	-	-	-
Subtotal	4,494	4,997	4,979	7,020	7,744	8,901	8,657
State budget[a]	-	-	-	-	-	-	45,800
Total (MNT million)	**4,494**	**4,997**	**4,979**	**7,020**	**7,744**	**8,901**	**54,457**
Exchange rate: US$1	1,824	1,935	1,973	2,339	2,450	2,620	2,620
Total (US$ million)	**$2.5**	**$2.6**	**$2.5**	**$3.0**	**$3.2**	**$3.4**	**$20.8**

[a] This is understood to include revenue from the gasoline and diesel tax and from the vehicle excise tax.
Sources: Financial audit reports 2014/15, 2016/17, 2019, and 2020.

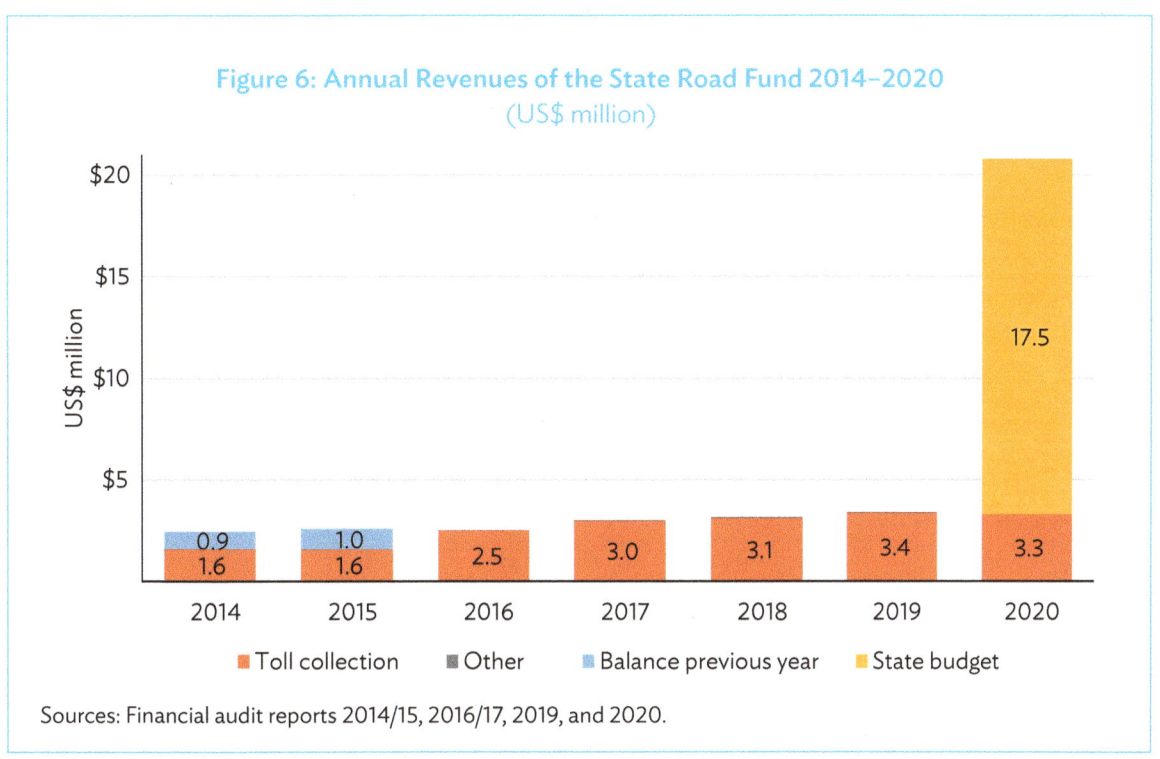

Figure 6: Annual Revenues of the State Road Fund 2014–2020 (US$ million)

Sources: Financial audit reports 2014/15, 2016/17, 2019, and 2020.

Revenue Allocation

Expenditure on operating costs has increased over the years, more than doubling between 2014 and 2020. A significant portion of the expenditure involves salary and social security contributions for staff of the road fund, and especially for staff working in the toll stations. In 2017, 138 staff were contracted by RTDC for toll collection, of whom 130 worked in the 24 toll stations. The salary costs alone continued to make up 26% of collected toll revenue in 2020 and, together with other operational costs, this added up to 35%. This did not include the construction of toll plazas, which in 2018 and 2019 formed between 50% and 65% of the budget line for "other operating costs" of the State Road Fund and used up most of the toll revenue.

Expenditure of the State Road Fund is reported only in terms of funds directly spent in the operation of the road fund. The funds spent on road maintenance and repair are not reported in detail, and are only indicated as a total sum transferred to RTDC or as capital expenditure. The exact nature of the works carried out with State Road Fund financing is not reported in the financial audit reports, and the transfers are represented as single consolidated amounts. Where previous years saw the available budget transferred to RTDC for maintenance and routine repair, the significant increase in revenue in 2020 was allocated entirely to capital expenditure works, with transfers to RTDC for maintenance and routine repair actually decreasing. Further insight into the use of the State Road Fund financing is necessary, and the actual use of the State Road Fund financing should be reported in the annual report. The year 2018 saw expenditure exceeding revenues by over MNT4 billion ($1.6 million), which was charged to balances in the State Road Fund account.

Table 30: Annual Expenditure of the State Road Fund 2014–2020
(MNT million)

Source	2014	2015	2016	2017	2018	2019	2020
Salaries and social security	826	851	989	1,653	2,006	1,873	2,253
Other operating costs	137	112	337	193	4,472	3,327	804
Transfer to RTDC	3,532	2,872	3,339	5,161	5,549	3,861	183
Projects (balance funds)	0	1,162	0	0	0	0	0
Capital expenditure	0	0	0	0	5	0	46,948
Non-operating costs	0	0	0	0	0	50	571
Total expenditure	4,494	4,997	4,665	7,007	12,032	9,111	50,759
Operational cash flow	-	-	314	14	(4,288)	(209)	3,698
Exchange rate: US$1	826	851	989	1,653	2,450	1,873	2,253
Total expenditure (US$ million)	**$2.5**	**$2.6**	**$2.4**	**$3.0**	**$4.9**	**$3.5**	**$19.4**

( ) = negative, RTDC = Road and Transport Development Center.
Sources: Financial audit reports 2014/15, 2016/17, 2019, and 2020.

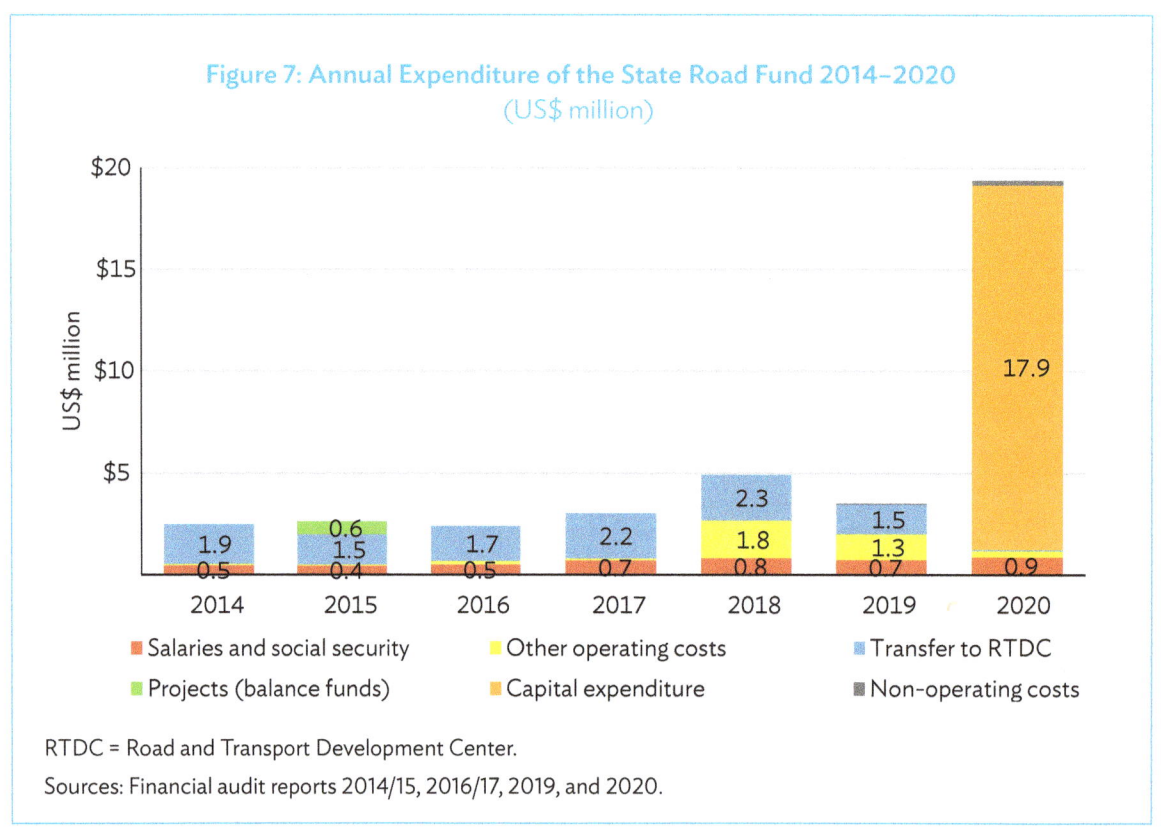

Figure 7: Annual Expenditure of the State Road Fund 2014–2020
(US$ million)

RTDC = Road and Transport Development Center.
Sources: Financial audit reports 2014/15, 2016/17, 2019, and 2020.

Funding Needs

The 2011 ADB report on Road Sector Development in Mongolia estimated that about $25 million per year was required to finance the maintenance and repair of the international and state road networks ($11 million for routine maintenance and repair and $14 million for regular repair). This assumed unit costs of $4,375/km/year for routine and regular repair of paved roads, $4,000/km/year for gravel roads, and an allocation of only $650/km/year for the earthen roads that make up the majority of international and state roads. A large length of international and national roads has been upgraded since then, however, requiring increased funding for their maintenance and repair. An updated funding needs assessment is required to take account of the changes to road network standards and conditions.

MRTD estimates the annual funding needs for road maintenance and repair that are to be funded through the State Road Fund to be in the order of MNT130 billion–MNT155 billion (about $50 million–$60 million). This does not include major repairs (rehabilitation) of roads with backlog maintenance, but does include costs not directly related to the annual implementation of works. Most of the cost is reserved for routine repair, which forms over 40% of the costs. This is closely followed by the costs related to the strengthening of the capacity of the AZZAs to carry out more and larger works through the procurement of plant and equipment, forming 25% of total estimated needs. The equipment and plant are mainly used for routine repairs, and thus further increases the budget allocated to this activity. Allocations to regular repair form only 15% of estimated needs, reflecting the low priority given to this type of activity by MTRD. The allocation to different maintenance and repair needs does not seem to reflect an optimal use of funding.

With the increased allocation of revenues from the gasoline and diesel tax and from the vehicle excise tax, revenue levels are currently in the order of $20 million. This is considered sufficient to cover the maintenance and the routine and emergency repair needs that are prioritized under the Law on Roads, and even allows a portion of the funding to be allocated to regular repairs (periodic maintenance) or major repairs (rehabilitation). Especially the financing of regular repairs is considered a priority in order to avoid further deterioration of the roads and reduce the need for costly rehabilitation in the future. However, Mongolia has a poor track record in carrying out regular repairs, with a total of only 18 km of regular repairs carried out in the period 2015–2017. With the significant increase in funding currently available from the State Road Fund, care will need to be taken that this does not only go to major repairs and equipment procurement, as currently appears to be happening with the significant allocation to capital expenditure. Although several efforts have been undertaken to develop a RAMS in Mongolia, this is not yet operational and is not forming the basis for annual planning and funding allocation. Such a RAMS could provide guidance in the allocation of the increased revenue of the State Road Fund, ensuring the optimization of benefits for road users resulting from the charges paid by them.

Table 31: Maintenance and Repair Needs
(MNT million)

Source	2020		2021		2022	
Maintenance (sweeping, snow clearance)	10,000	7.6%	12,000	8.4%	14,000	9.0%
Routine repair	58,500	44.6%	60,500	42.5%	62,500	40.1%
Emergency repair	7,500	5.7%	8,500	6.0%	10,000	6.4%
Regular repair (periodic maintenance)	19,800	15.1%	21,160	14.9%	23,800	15.3%
Subtotal	**95,800**	**73.0%**	**102,160**	**71.8%**	**110,300**	**70.8%**
Research	230	0.2%	250	0.2%	280	0.2%
Traffic data collection	210	0.2%	200	0.1%	190	0.1%
Condition surveys	100	0.1%	100	0.1%	950	0.6%
Mobile patrols	160	0.1%	190	0.1%	230	0.1%
Independent inspection	1,600	1.2%	1,700	1.2%	1,800	1.2%
Toll plazas	910	0.7%	1,500	1.1%	1,800	1.2%
Equipment and technology upgrading	100	0.1%	90	0.1%	80	0.1%
Heavy vehicle overload control	48	0.04%	58	0.04%	69	0.04%
Information for road users	26	0.02%	28	0.02%	31	0.02%
Strengthening industrial capacity	32,000	24.4%	36,000	25.3%	40,000	25.7%
Education and training	33	0.03%	36	0.03%	40	0.03%
Subtotal	**35,417**	**27.0%**	**40,152**	**28.2%**	**45,470**	**29.2%**
Total	**131,217**	**100.0%**	**142,312**	**100.0%**	**155,770**	**100.0%**
Exchange rate: US$1	2,061		2,061		2,061	
Total (US$ million)	**$50.1**		**$54.3**		**$59.5**	

Source: ADB. 2021. *Technical Assistance to Mongolia for Policy Advice and Capacity Building on Road Maintenance and Asset Management*. Manila (TA9544-MON).

PAKISTAN

Pakistan has 13,570 km of roads that are classified as national highways, including 78 km of expressways, 2,066 km of motorways, and 11,426 km of general highways. The national highways are managed by the National Highway Authority (NHA), which was created in 1991 under the Ministry of Communications (MOC) through the NHA Act. NHA is responsible for planning, development, operation, repair, and maintenance of national highways and strategic roads entrusted to NHA by the federal government or by the provincial governments. It is managed by a National Highways Council and an NHA Executive Board. All roadworks are tendered out competitively to the private sector.

Road Fund Management

The Road Maintenance Account (RMA) was established through the 2003 NHA Road Maintenance Account Rules issued by the MOC with reference to the 1991 NHA Act that gives the NHA the right to collect certain road user charges and credit these to the National Highway Authority Fund managed by NHA. The RMA is a special account under that fund, reserved specifically for maintenance and rehabilitation. The NHA Code was updated in 2005 to reflect the main elements of the RMA. SOPs for the RMA were prepared in 2002 and updated in 2005. Road funds have been established also in some states, but these are not treated in this document. Funding for these state-level road funds has been an issue, as tolling is a less-suitable funding source for state-level roads compared to the national highways and expressways financed through the RMA, and other possible funding sources have only limited revenues.

Eligible Activities

The 2005 NHA Code and RMA SOPs distinguish between routine maintenance (pothole patching, crack sealing, drainage cleaning, vegetation control, etc.); periodic maintenance (chip seals, asphalt overlays, structure repairs, etc.); emergency maintenance (ensuring safety and traffic flow after landslides, flooding, heavy snowfall, and accidents); rehabilitation (thick overlays, replacement of structural layers, major repairs, or replacement of structures); and the so-called geometric improvements (involving reconstruction with changes to width, curvature, alignment, and gradient of roads and structures). The SOPs define that at least 85% of the RMA revenues must be used for routine and periodic maintenance or rehabilitation of existing network assets. The remaining 15% of annual RMA revenues may be used for geometric improvements (up to 6%), safety improvements (up to 5%), new toll plazas (up to 2.5%), and corridor management (up to 1.5%).[9] Allocation of available funding will be prioritized according to

---

[9] This includes the management of the right-of-way; roadside facilities (rest areas, service stations, etc.); traffic and highway safety operations (awareness campaigns, enforcement of traffic laws, roadside emergency services, etc.); and weigh and toll station operations.

the order of eligible activities as listed in Table 32, with first priority to be given to routine and periodic maintenance. All activities are to be procured through competitive contracting procedures. RMA funds may not be used for other purposes or for bridging funding gaps for non-eligible expenditures.

Up until 2010, the RMA operated well, focusing on financing maintenance, with up to 60% of funding allocated to periodic maintenance. In 2010, part of the funding was diverted to construction projects. That year also saw over 1,000 km of highways damaged by flooding and requiring emergency maintenance. The result was that periodic maintenance was hardly carried out over a period of 2 years. After 2012, an extensive periodic maintenance program was launched covering 1,600 km of highways over a period of 3 years.

Table 32: Activities Eligible for Financing from the Road Maintenance Account

- Routine maintenance
- Periodic maintenance
- Emergency maintenance
- Rehabilitation
- Safety improvements
- Geometric improvements
- Toll plazas
- Corridor management

Sources: 2005 NHA Code, and 2005 Road Maintenance Account Standard Operating Procedures.

Management Structure

The management of the RMA involves various entities. Day-to-day management regarding the implementation of works financed from RMA funding is carried out by the Road Asset Management Division (RAMD) under the Operations Wing of NHA. The financial management of revenues and expenditures of the RMA account is carried out by the Revenues and Accounts Division under the Finance Wing of NHA.

In addition, there is a range of committees and boards that play different roles in the management of the RMA. The RMA Technical Scrutiny Part is responsible for reviewing the technical aspects of the Annual Maintenance Plan (AMP) that is to be financed from the RMA, and for verifying the cost estimates. The RMA Steering Committee is subsequently responsible for reviewing the AMP and ensuring it corresponds to the priorities of the country. The final approval of the AMP and the funding allocation from the RMA is by the NHA chair and subsequently the NHA Executive Board. Individual projects within the AMP also need approval before they can be implemented. Projects of up to PRs20 million (about $110,000) can be approved by the general manager of the NHA Operations Wing, while larger projects of up to PRs50 million need approval of the member (head) of the NHA Operations Wing. The NHA chair can approve projects of up to PRs100 million (about $565,000), while projects exceeding PRs100 million require approval by the NHA Executive Board. Larger periodic maintenance and rehabilitation projects thus need approval from the NHA Executive Board.

The members of the different boards and committees are listed in Table 33. The RMA Technical Scrutiny Party mainly consists of representatives of different sections of NHA, as well as of the National Highway and Motorway Police (NHMP) and the National Transport Research Centre (NTRC), all of which fall under MOC. The RMA Steering Committee has one representative from the Planning Commission, with all others from MOC and underlying NHA, NHMP and NTRC. The NHA Executive Board again has all its members from MOC or underlying NHA, NHMP and NTRC, except for one representative from the National Engineering Service Pakistan, a government-owned consultancy company. Although local consultations are carried out as part of the planning process, there are no road user representatives in any of the boards involved in the approval of the annual work plan. The management structure of the RMA is presented in Figure 8.

Table 33: Members of the National Highway Authority and the Road Maintenance Account Management Entities

NHA Executive Board	RMA Steering Committee	RMA Technical Scrutiny Party
• NHA chair • NHMP inspector general • NHA additional secretary (finance) • NHA member or additional secretary (Planning & Development Division) • MOC joint secretary (II) • NTRC senior chief/chief • NESPAK (vice-) president • NHA member (finance) • NHA member (planning)	• NHA member (operations) • MOC joint secretary • NHA member (finance) • NHA member (planning) • Planning commission chief (transport and communications) • NHMP representative • NTRC deputy chief • NHA general manager (operations)	• NHA general manager (operations) • NHA general manager (finance) • NHA general manager (planning and design) • NHA general manager (contracts) • NHA general managers, regional offices • NHMP representative • NTRC representative • NHA director (Road Asset Management Division)

MOC = Ministry of Communications, NESPAK = National Engineering Services Pakistan, NHA = National Highway Authority, NHMP = National Highway and Motorway Police, NTRC = National Transport Research Centre.

Source: National Highway Authority Code, 2005.

Funding Approval and Allocation

RAMD is responsible for preparing an AMP and corresponding budget using NHA's RAMS and through consultations with the NHA regional offices. The AMP only includes maintenance activities (routine, periodic and emergency maintenance) and small improvement works financed from the RMA. Preparation of the AMP was initially carried out by RAMD staff, but is now outsourced to private consultants in combination with the data collection for the RAMS under 3-year contracts. The collected data is stored in the RAMS database and is analyzed using HDM4 software to determine maintenance needs and optimize the use of available funding.

The draft AMP is first reviewed by the Technical Scrutiny Party to verify that the proposed works are technically justified and that their cost estimates are in order. This includes representatives from the different wings of NHA as well as from the relevant regional offices of NHA. Subsequently the AMP is reviewed by the RMA Steering Committee with higher level representatives of NHA as well as from the

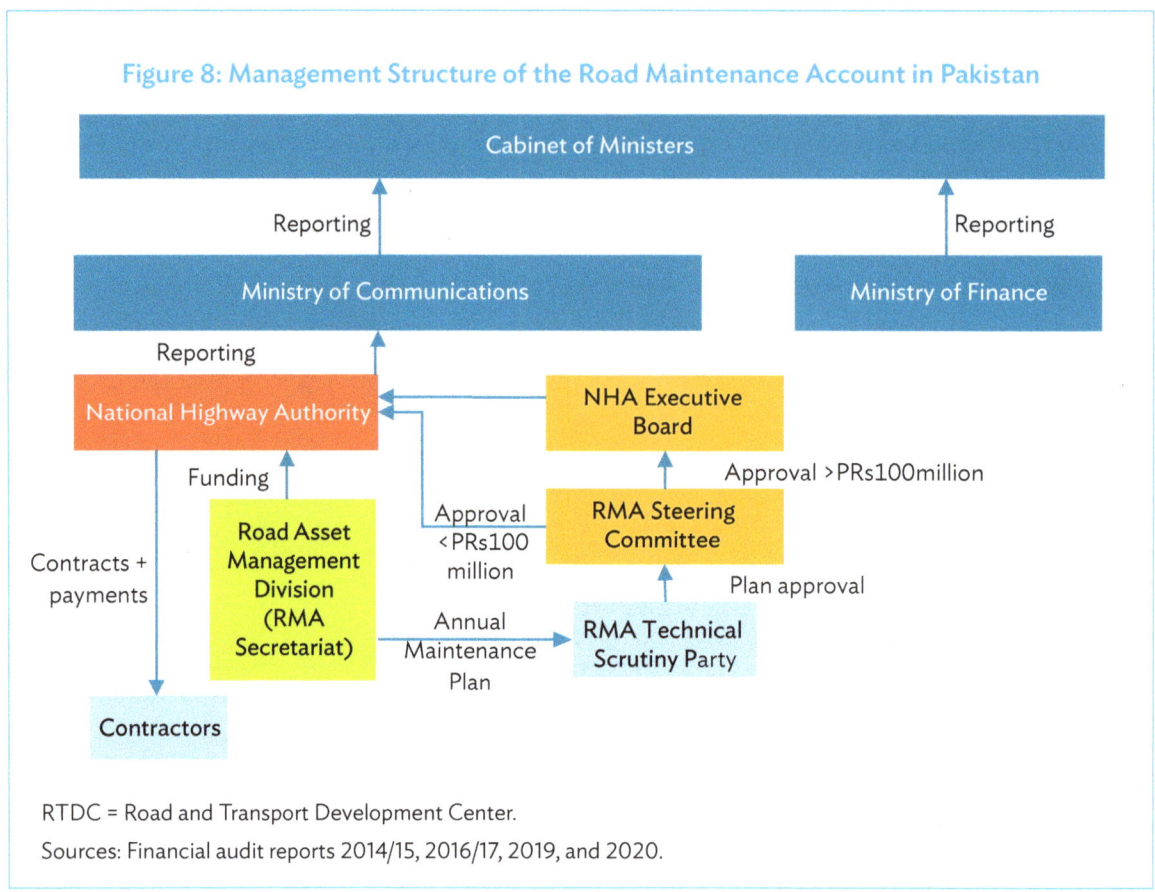

Figure 8: Management Structure of the Road Maintenance Account in Pakistan

RTDC = Road and Transport Development Center.
Sources: Financial audit reports 2014/15, 2016/17, 2019, and 2020.

MOC, the National Highways and Motorway Police, the NTRC, and the Planning Commission. After approval by the Steering Committee, the AMP is forwarded for approval by the NHA Chairman or the NHA Executive Board depending on the size of the contracts concerned.

Payments for works carried out with RMA funds are made by the Revenues and Accounts Directorate after receiving certification from the engineer/project manager that the works, goods or services have been carried out and delivered according to specifications. The Revenues and Accounts Directorate verifies that invoices have been certified, guarantees are still valid, deductions have been applied, and fund allocations are conformed with. Payments to the contractors are made directly from the RMA bank accounts. For small contracts and operational costs of the NHA regional offices, transfers are made to the RMA accounts in each of the regions, and payments may be made directly from these accounts.

Financial and Technical Accountability

The RMA is set up as a non-lapsable account in Pakistani commercial banks. The RMA is an off-budget road fund, where all the revenues are collected by NHA (or collection is outsourced by NHA) and deposited directly into the RMA bank account. The revenues do not go through the Federal Budget and are not included in or approved as part of the annual budgeting system.

As part of the preparation of the AMP for the subsequent year, RAMD is required to present and discuss the planned activities during structured consultations with 50–60 road user representatives in each of the regions. These consultations allow feedback and comments to be obtained from local road users regarding the proposed maintenance activities prioritized using HDM4. The RMA SOPs include terms of reference for carrying out stakeholder consultations.

At the end of the financial year, RAMD is required to prepare an annual report with details of the RAMS analysis carried out and the subsequent preparation of the AMP and its discussion in regional consultations. The report also provides a summary of the review by the Technical Scrutiny Party and the Steering Committee and the final approval of the AMP. The annual report further describes the subsequent procurement of works, goods and services and the implementation of the AMP, and the achievement of targets. The Revenues and Accounts Directorate of NHA is required to prepare the balance sheet, statement of income and expenditure, and the statement of cash flow, submitting these together with the annual report prepared by RAMD to the NHA Executive Board for approval.

The NHA Code requires that a firm of chartered accountants is hired by the NHA Executive Board to audit the financial statements and the annual report of the RMA on an annual basis. The NHA Executive Board is further required to hire a firm or individual on a regular basis to carry out a technical audit of the activities financed by the RMA. The audit reports need to verify the completeness of the RMA revenue levels, the correctness of the rates applied, the conformity of payments with eligible expenditures and priorities, and the accuracy of accounting, among other things. The RMA SOPs provide sample terms of reference for financial and technical audits, including an outline of the auditor reports. The annual report prepared by RAMD, together with the audited financial statement and the auditor's report, is forwarded to the auditor general of Pakistan and published on the NHA website, and printed copies are to be made available in head office and regional offices of NHA.

In addition to the audits of the RMA, the NHA as a whole is also required to prepare an annual report and financial statements, and to have these audited by the auditor general on an annual basis. Since the RMA forms part of the NHA, the RMA is also included in the NHA audit.

Road Fund Revenue

Past attempts to establish an independent road fund financed from fuel taxes were not successful because of disagreements about the sharing of revenues between the federal government and the states. A decision was therefore made to instead focus on road user charges already collected by the MOC and its underlying entities, of which the revenue could easily be earmarked for the RMA. As a result, the earmarked revenues are off-budget, collected by NHA and other entities under MOC, and deposited directly into the RMA account.

Revenue Sources

The RMA Rules identify the following road user charges as revenues of the RMA (net of collection costs). In practice, however, revenues are only received from tolls, traffic fines, axle load charges, and charges for the use of the right-of-way. These fees and charges are collected directly by NHA or other entities under the MOC. The RAMD is responsible for regularly reviewing the rates and proposing adjustments to meet the maintenance needs. Proposed adjustments of the rates are reviewed and approved by the NHA Executive Board, and are published in national newspapers.

Table 34: Sources of Funding of the Road Maintenance Account

- Tolls on roads and bridges
- Traffic fines on highways and motorways (overloading, traffic fines, etc.)
- Charges for commercial use of the right-of-way
- Axle load charges (weigh station fees)
- Supplementary heavy vehicle fee
- International transit fee
- Border fee
- Allocations from the federal government
- International loans and grants[a]

[a] Although mentioned in the 2005 National Highway Authority Code, this was never applied in practice.
Source: National Highway Authority Code, 2005.

Tolls on roads and bridges. Tolls were first introduced in 1999. Toll collection is regulated by the NHA Act that allows NHA to collect tolls on national highways and bridges. Toll rates are defined by NHA and are approved by the NHA Executive Board and published in the national press and website of NHA. Different toll rates are applied for closed-entry motorways (total 1,570 km) and open-entry highways. The toll rates per kilometer for the motorways are listed in Table 35 and range from just under $0.01 per kilometer for cars to nearly $0.05 per kilometer for heavy trucks.

Toll collection is managed by the assistant director tolls under the general manager revenue in the Finance Wing of NHA. Actual implementation of the toll collection is contracted out by NHA to so-called operation and management contractors. These are service contracts with agreed payments for the collection of the tolls (risk of toll revenue is with NHA), or as a maximum guaranteed bid with lump sum payments to the RMA by the contractor in exchange for being allowed to collect the toll (risk of toll revenue is with the contractor). Contracts are generally for one financial year (July–June). In cases where toll collection contracts are terminated or cannot be awarded, toll collection is carried out directly by NHA.

Traffic fines. Revenue collection from fines is managed by the assistant director weigh station/police fines under the general manager revenue in the Finance Wing of NHA. Issuing of the fines and collection of the payments is carried out by the NHMP. The NHMP falls under the Ministry of Construction and operates in the motorways and highways managed by NHA. The revenues from the fines, net of collection costs, are transferred to the RMA account. In 2019–2020, a total of 9.6 million fines were issued by the NHMP, down from 11.1 million the year before.

Table 35: Motorway Toll Rates
(US$/km)

Motorway	Length (km)	Car	Bus <12 Seats	Bus 13–24 Seats	Bus >24 Seats	2- or 3-Axle Truck	Articulated Truck
M1 Islamabad-Peshawar	161	$0.009	$0.014	$0.020	$0.028	$0.037	$0.045
M3 Lahore-M4	228	$0.010	$0.014	$0.021	$0.030	$0.039	$0.048
M4 Pindi Bhattia-Shorkot	176	$0.010	$0.014	$0.021	$0.030	$0.039	$0.048
M4 Shorkot-Sher Shah	121	$0.010	$0.014	$0.021	$0.030	$0.039	$0.048
M5 Start-Shershah	392	$0.010	$0.014	$0.021	$0.030	$0.039	$0.048
M14 Hakla-DI Khan	293	$0.009	$0.014	$0.020	$0.028	$0.037	$0.045
E35/M15 Hasan Abdal-Manshera	100	$0.007	$0.012	$0.017	$0.025	$0.032	$0.039

km = kilometer.
Source: National Highway Authority website.

Charges for commercial use of the right-of-way. Collection of charges for commercial use of the right-of-way in motorways and highways is managed by the assistant director right-of-way under the general manager revenue in the Finance Wing of NHA. In 2009, the NHA issued SOPs for leasing of the right-of-way that aim to commercialize the right-of-way and develop it as an important source of income for the RMA. Currently, NHA is faced with encroachment and unauthorized use of the right-of-way and has started mapping buildings and other structures in an effort to regulate the usage of the right-of-way. NHA is also facing old leases that were signed by the provincial construction and works departments before the NHA was created, and that provide certain entities with the right to use the right-of-way at no or very little cost, often with very long lease periods of 99 years (600 cases are reported by NHA). NHA aims to regulate these existing leases and introduce short-term leases for new service stations and other amenities.

Revenue Levels

The RMA is largely dependent on toll revenue, which provided PRs25.6 billion ($145 million) in 2019–2020, equivalent to 64% of total RMA revenue. The length of motorways and highways under tolls continues to expand, but is limited by the available network. Over time, the portion of the total RMA revenue received from tolling is gradually dropping (from 80% in 2014–2015 to 64% in 2019–2020), with other revenues increasing more rapidly. Total revenue of the RMA has doubled since 2014–2015 in Pakistan rupee terms, reaching nearly PRs40 billion in 2019–2020 ($225 million). RMA revenues have developed less dramatically in US dollar terms, increasing by 34% over this same period. The RMA revenue levels are presented in Table 36 in Pakistan rupees, and in Figure 9 in US dollars.

Table 36: Actual Revenues of the Road Maintenance Account 2014–2021
(PRs million)

Source	2014/15	2015/16	2016/17	2017/18	2018/19	2019/20	2020/21[a]
Tolls	15,544	15,556	18,804	19,298	23,052	25,669	14,291
Police fines	1,819	573	3,908	4,015	4,168	4,113	2,462
Right-of-way	306	2,274	1,225	1,913	1,911	2,307	1,292
Weigh station	223	390	345	541	449	617	535
BOT revenue	0	0	0	0	86	0	0
Other	1,490	1,201	397	2,078	3,102	7,170	3,036
Total (PRs million)	**19,382**	**19,994**	**24,679**	**27,845**	**32,768**	**39,876**	**21,616**
Exchange rate	100.2	103.9	103.5	110.2	138.6	154.2	159.8
Total (US$ million)	**$193.5**	**$192.4**	**$238.5**	**$252.6**	**$236.4**	**$258.7**	**$244.3**

BOT = build–operate–transfer.

[a] Up to December 2020.

Sources: Auditor general audit reports.

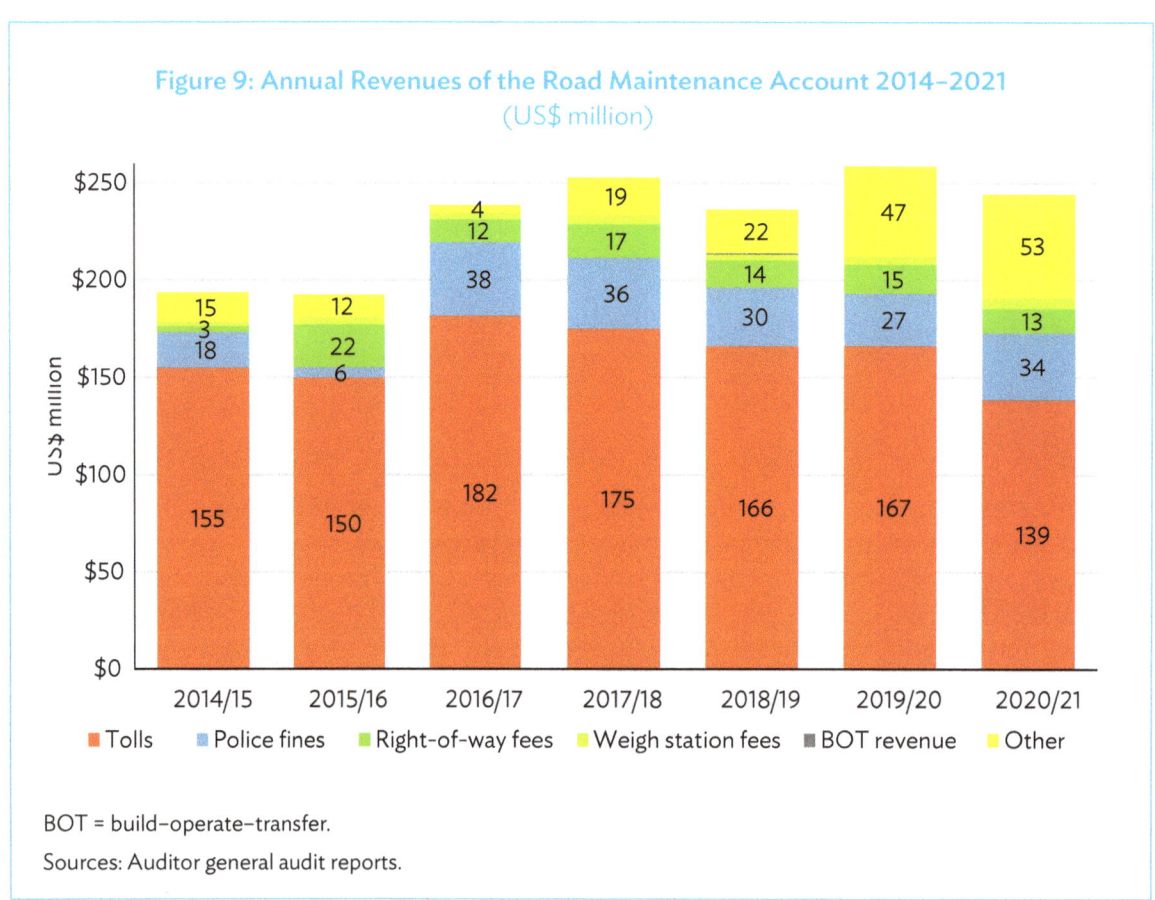

Figure 9: Annual Revenues of the Road Maintenance Account 2014–2021
(US$ million)

BOT = build–operate–transfer.
Sources: Auditor general audit reports.

Revenue Allocation

The annual allocation of RMA funding is defined in the AMP, which is approved by NHA. The AMPs for the past 4 years are presented in Table 37. The main expenditure item is periodic maintenance, which takes up half the available funding. This is followed by routine maintenance that averages about 17% of RMA funding and various other types of maintenance that take up nearly 10% of funding. Noteworthy is the special maintenance, which involves localized backlog maintenance, especially for new highways that are transferred from the states to the authority of NHA. Rehabilitation on average takes up 10% of available funding and mainly involves roads that have reached the end of their life span. Geometric improvements, safety improvements, toll plazas, and corridor management tend to remain below the thresholds set in the RMA SOPs. Administrative expenses and other expenses related to the management of the highway network form 7% of the AMP budget on average, despite not being expressly mentioned as eligible expenditures in the RMA SOPs.

Table 37: Annual Planned Expenditure of the Road Maintenance Account 2017–2021
(PRs million)

Expenditure Item	2017/18		2018/19		2019/20		2020/21	
Routine maintenance	5,187	19.0%	5,292	16.0%	6,047	17.5%	6,890	16.2%
Periodic maintenance	13,032	47.8%	15,280	46.2%	16,262	47.0%	21,233	49.9%
Emergency maintenance	500	1.8%	500	1.5%	500	1.4%	500	1.2%
Special maintenance	1,500	5.5%	1,200	3.6%	2,300	6.6%	3,000	7.0%
Bridge and culvert maintenance	600	2.2%	500	1.5%	600	1.7%	1,000	2.3%
Preventive maintenance/ slope stability	325	1.2%	200	0.6%	200	0.6%	100	0.2%
Rehabilitation	2,199	8.1%	5,445	16.4%	3,049	8.8%	3,448	8.1%
Geometric improvements	200	0.7%	200	0.6%	600	1.7%	700	1.6%
Highway safety	1,000	3.7%	1,260	3.8%	850	2.5%	1,156	2.7%
Toll plazas and weigh stations	600	2.2%	900	2.7%	850	2.5%	900	2.1%
Corridor management	100	0.4%	100	0.3%	500	1.4%	700	1.6%
Afforestation along highways	100	0.4%	100	0.3%	100	0.3%	100	0.2%
Administrative expenses	1,650	6.1%	1,500	4.5%	1,500	4.3%	1,500	3.5%
Logistic expenses/survey equipment	90	0.3%	200	0.6%	200	0.6%	200	0.5%
Consultancies	100	0.4%	350	1.1%	650	1.9%	700	1.6%
Other	80	0.3%	80	0.2%	415	1.2%	440	1.0%
Total	27,263	100.0%	33,106	100.0%	34,623	100.0%	42,567	100.0%
Exchange rate: US$1	110.2		138.6		154.2		159.8	
Total (US$ million)	$247.3		$238.9		$224.6		$266.4	

Sources: Annual maintenance plans 2017/18 – 2020/21.

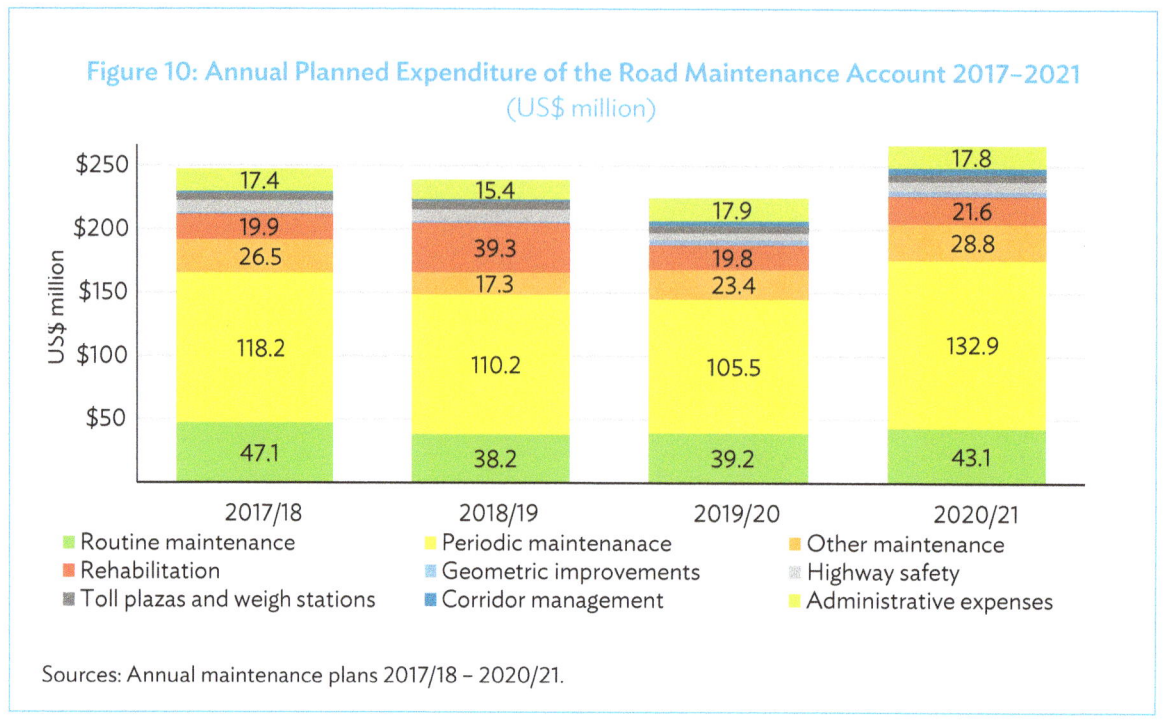

Figure 10: Annual Planned Expenditure of the Road Maintenance Account 2017–2021 (US$ million)

Sources: Annual maintenance plans 2017/18 – 2020/21.

Funding Needs

NHA uses HDM4 to determine its maintenance and rehabilitation needs, starting with an unconstrained budget analysis to determine the optimal needs. This is followed by a constrained analysis where the expected RMA revenue is taken as the upper limit of the budget, with the allocation optimized to maximize economic benefits. In 2003–2004, the optimal funding needs were determined to be just under PRs7 billion ($125 million). Over time, the needs grew to PRs64 billion in 2019–2020 ($415 million).[10] To a large extent, this is because of the expansion of the road length under the responsibility of NHA, as state highways were transferred to NHA that was considered to be in a better position to finance their maintenance than the state governments. The upgrading and new construction of motorways have also led to increased funding needs.

At the same time, RMA revenue growth has not been able to keep up with demand. Where the RMA revenue was able to cover over 70% of needs at the time of establishment, coverage gradually decreased to 40%–50% in past years. This is forming a considerable problem, with highways receiving insufficient maintenance and becoming subject to accelerated deterioration. The inclusion of some state highways under the responsibility of NHA led to a worsening of road conditions as reflected in the average roughness of the network in Figure 11. Many of the poor highways have since been improved through capital investments financed outside of the RMA, resulting in a gradual improvement in network conditions. The improved road conditions have also reduced the maintenance funding needs, although these remain nearly twice as high as the available funding from the RMA. Most high-volume highways and motorways have now been put under tolling and, although some additional road sections can still be tolled and provide additional revenue, this is very limited. Although toll rates are relatively low in

---

[10] Needs in earlier years were even higher in United States dollar terms, reaching $530 million in 2016–2017.

Pakistan, increases to the toll rates are not considered a viable option because toll roads already have relatively low usage in Pakistan, and it is expected that road users will opt to use non-tolled highways. NHA is now looking at increasing its revenues from the use of the right-of-way, but this is unlikely to provide the necessary levels of revenue and additional sources of funding will need to be identified.

Table 38: Maintenance Needs and Approved Plans

Financial Year	Needs (PRs million)	AMP budget (PRs million)	Coverage	Exchange Rate (US$1)	Needs (US$ million)	AMP budget (US$ million)
2003/04	6,986	4,989	71%	55.3	126.3	90.2
2004/05	7,000	5,713	82%	59.4	117.9	96.2
2005/06	10,500	7,430	71%	59.8	175.7	124.3
2006/07	14,000	6,839	49%	60.9	229.9	112.3
2007/08	14,316	8,414	59%	61.3	233.5	137.3
2008/09	15,782	10,650	67%	78.8	200.4	135.2
2009/10	18,961	13,000	69%	83.8	226.3	155.1
2010/11	25,091	19,759	79%	85.3	294.3	231.7
2011/12	28,572	17,314	61%	89.6	319.1	193.3
2012/13	28,000	13,750	49%	97.2	288.1	141.5
2013/14	40,350	17,930	44%	105.1	383.8	170.5
2014/15	45,000	23,360	52%	100.2	449.2	233.2
2015/16	51,000	22,773	45%	103.9	490.7	219.1
2016/17	55,000	23,761	43%	103.5	531.4	229.6
2017/18	58,000	27,263	47%	110.2	526.2	247.3
2018/19	60,000	33,106	55%	138.6	432.9	238.9
2019/20	64,000	34,493	54%	154.2	415.2	223.7

AMP = Annual Maintenance Plan.
Source: National Highway Authority.

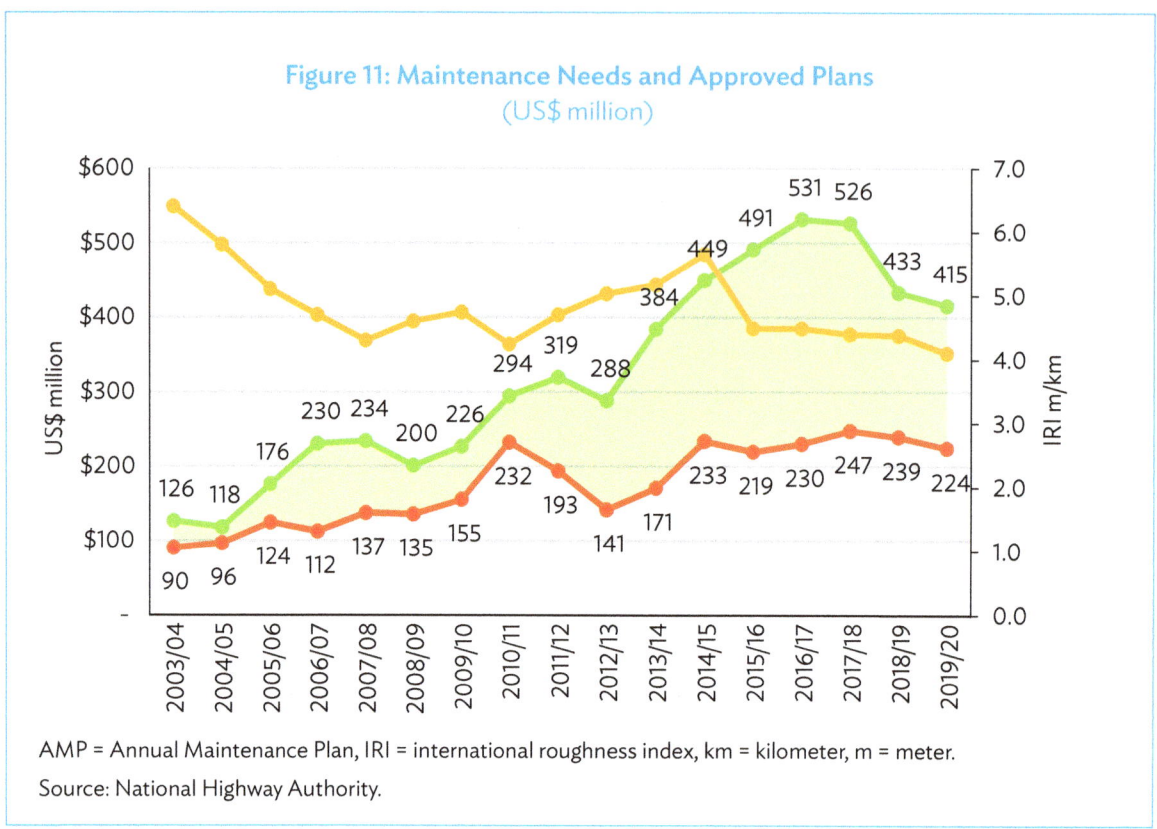

Figure 11: Maintenance Needs and Approved Plans (US$ million)

AMP = Annual Maintenance Plan, IRI = international roughness index, km = kilometer, m = meter.
Source: National Highway Authority.

UZBEKISTAN

Uzbekistan has 42,869 km of public roads, including 3,993 km of international roads, 14,203 km of national roads, and 24,673 km of local roads. The institutional responsibilities for these roads have been subject to considerable reform since independence. In 1993, the then Ministry of Highways was transformed into the state joint stock concern *Uzavtodor*, which was a voluntary association of state-owned construction and maintenance enterprises that together were responsible for the construction and maintenance of roads. In 2003, *Uzavtodor* was transformed into the state joint stock company *Uzavtoyul* and made responsible for managing the construction, repair, and maintenance of roads, entering into contracts with the individual construction and maintenance enterprises for the implementation of works. In 2017, *Uzavtoyul* was transformed into the State Committee for Roads as a legal entity with an independent balance sheet, accountable to the Cabinet of Ministers, and with the construction and maintenance enterprises as subordinate entities. In 2019, the Ministry of Transport (MOT) was created, and the State Committee for Roads was transformed into the Committee for Roads and placed under MOT. This also introduced a partial separation of client and contractor functions, introducing contractual relationships with subordinate maintenance enterprises (with salary and operating costs included in the contract amount), corporatizing and later privatizing a number of construction enterprises, and requiring that road construction and capital repair contracts be tendered competitively and opened up to participation by the private sector.

The Committee for Roads is now responsible for the management of the public road network. The 13 Regional Road Departments under the Committee for Roads are responsible for managing the maintenance and current repair of public roads through the different maintenance enterprises set up as unitary enterprises under the Regional Road Departments. This includes 39 corridor maintenance enterprises, 161 district road maintenance enterprises, 5 specialized road maintenance enterprises, and 13 bridge maintenance enterprises. Other subordinate entities of the Committee for Roads include the state unitary enterprise (SUE) Directorate for the Construction and Reconstruction of Public Roads that is responsible for procuring (re)construction and capital repair works for public roads, the SUE Corporate Services for Regional Roads that is responsible for contracting works in rural and urban roads under the authority of regional governments, the unitary enterprise Landscaping responsible for managing the right-of-way in public roads, the *Avtoyulinvest* Agency that is responsible for managing projects funded by development partners, and about 30 other enterprises.

Road Fund Management

Uzbekistan first introduced road funds in 1993 through Resolution #334. This included a Republican Road Fund (RRF) under *Uzavtodor* as well as regional road funds under the regional state joint stock associations and local road funds under the district road administrations. These were set up as simple bank accounts under the entities concerned and received earmarked revenues.

The 2003 Decree #3292 that converted *Uzavtodor* into *Uzavtoyul* also liquidated the different road funds and transferred the assets to a new RRF under the Ministry of Finance. Regulations for the RRF were issued through the 2003 Resolution #361 of the Cabinet of Ministers. In 2017, Decree #4954 placed RRF directly under the Cabinet of Ministers, with Resolution #222 of the Cabinet of Ministers providing updated regulations for RRF.

In 2019, the RRF was abolished through Decree #4086, and its balances were transferred to the state budget. Decree #4545 identified *Avtoyulinvest* Agency as the legal successor of RRF, establishing it as a separate legal entity under the Committee for Roads that acts as an executive body for the implementation of road sector investment projects with participation of international financial institutions and foreign governmental financial institutions. However, *Avtoyulinvest* is no longer involved in domestic funding of the road sector as its predecessor RRF used to be.

Instead, the 2019 Decree #5890 created a new Republican Trust Fund for Road Development (Republican Fund), with regulations approved through the 2020 Resolution #123 of the Cabinet of Ministers. In addition, the decree created a total of 14 Regional Trust Funds for Road Development (regional funds) under the governments of the Republic of Karakalpakstan, the 12 regions, and the capital city Tashkent. The 2019 Resolution #924 of the Cabinet of Ministers further created a specific Fund for the Development and Support of the Activities of the Committee for Roads, which directly funds the operational costs of the Committee for Roads and some of its subordinate enterprises.

Eligible Activities

Uzbekistan has a specific definition of road activities, where routine and periodic maintenance have been merged. Resolution #226 of 2006 distinguishes between maintenance (including landscaping, winter maintenance, and summer maintenance); current repair (small pavement and structure repairs); midterm repair (periodic maintenance involving renewal of the wearing course); capital repair (rehabilitation); and (re)construction. In 2011, the resolution was updated, however, and midterm repair was merged with current repair, covering both routine pavement and structure repairs as well as (partial) renewal of the wearing course.

The RRF established in 2003 funded design, construction, reconstruction, repair, maintenance, and the procurement of equipment for public roads, in the same way as the 1993 funds had done. The RRF regulations also determined that RRF funding could be used to finance the operation of the RRF secretariat, and to cover the operational costs of *Uzavtoyul* and its subsidiary enterprises, as well as its successor, the State Committee for Roads. A State Inspectorate for Quality Control of Road Construction Works was established under the Cabinet of Ministers in that same year, which was also financed from RRF revenues.

The Republican Fund that replaced the RRF in 2019 continues to finance the design, construction, reconstruction, repair, and maintenance of public roads, while the regional funds finance the design, construction, reconstruction, repair, and maintenance of urban and rural roads. The Republican Fund regulations also allow funding to be used to finance the development of a RAMS and related geographic information system mapping of the road network. The Republican Fund further finances the staff salaries of the Committee for Roads, its 13 Regional Road Departments, SUE Customer Service for Regional

Roads, unitary enterprise Center for Information and Communication Technologies, unitary enterprise Republican Dispatch Center, unitary enterprise Landscaping, and *Avtoyulinvest* Agency. A separate Fund for the Development and Support of the Activities of the Committee for Roads serves to finance staff incentives and the operational costs of these entities. Other entities under the Committee for Roads are financed directly through the contracts signed with them.

Table 39: Activities Eligible for Financing from the Republican Road Fund and Subsequent Republican Fund

- Design
- Winter and summer maintenance
- Current repair (including midterm repair)
- Capital repair
- Construction and reconstruction
- Equipment procurement
- Operation of secretariat
- Operation of Uzavtoyul/State Committee for Roads/Committee for Roads and subsidiary enterprises
- Operation of State Inspectorate for Quality Control of Road Construction Works
- Road asset management system and geographic information system mapping

Sources: Republican Road Fund and Republican Fund regulations.

Management Structure

In 2003, the RRF was set up as a separate legal entity under the Ministry of Finance and made responsible for financial management of the RRF. In 2006, the RRF was also made responsible for preparing investment projects and tender documents for construction, reconstruction, and repair works and for acting as the client for these works. As such, it became responsible for managing the implementation of roadworks in addition to the financial management. Maintenance and current repair were also financed by the RRF, but implementation was managed by *Uzavtoyul* and its underlying enterprises. This changed in 2017 with the transformation of *Uzavtoyul* into the State Committee for Roads, which again became the client for all domestically funded works. The RRF continued to be responsible for managing the implementation of road projects financed by development partners, acting as the executing agency. With the abolishment of the RRF in 2019, the responsibility for managing development partner projects was transferred to its successor, *Avtoyulinvest* Agency, while the responsibility for funding and financial management was transferred to the Republican Fund and the regional funds.

The 2003 RRF regulations established an Executive Directorate with 45 staff positions to function as secretariat. The executive director of the RRF was originally appointed by the Cabinet of Ministers at the proposal of the minister of finance, and held a position equal to that of a deputy minister. Deputy directors were appointed by the minister of finance, with agreement of the RRF Management Board. This was later changed, with the executive director appointed by the Cabinet of Ministers with the approval of the President, and deputy directors appointed by the executive director with approval of the Cabinet of Ministers. Other staff of the Executive Directorate was appointed directly by the executive director.

The RRF Management Board was also established through the 2003 regulations of the RRF. This 13-member Management Board was responsible for approving spending by the RRF based on road development and improvement programs and road maintenance and repair plans presented by the RRF Executive Directorate and *Uzavtoyul*. The RRF Management Board was also responsible for monitoring revenue transfers to the RRF and for making proposals for improving revenue collection for the RRF. In 2017, the RRF was placed under the Cabinet of Ministers and new regulations were approved. These stipulated that reports by the Executive Directorate on the use of funding would not only be presented to the Management Board, but also to representatives of the Ministry of Economy, the Ministry of Finance, the State Architectural Construction of the Republic of Uzbekistan, the State Committee for Roads, and the State Inspectorate for Quality Control of Road Construction Works. The new regulations also stipulated that the Management Board would meet at least once every quarter, with decision-making through a simple majority.

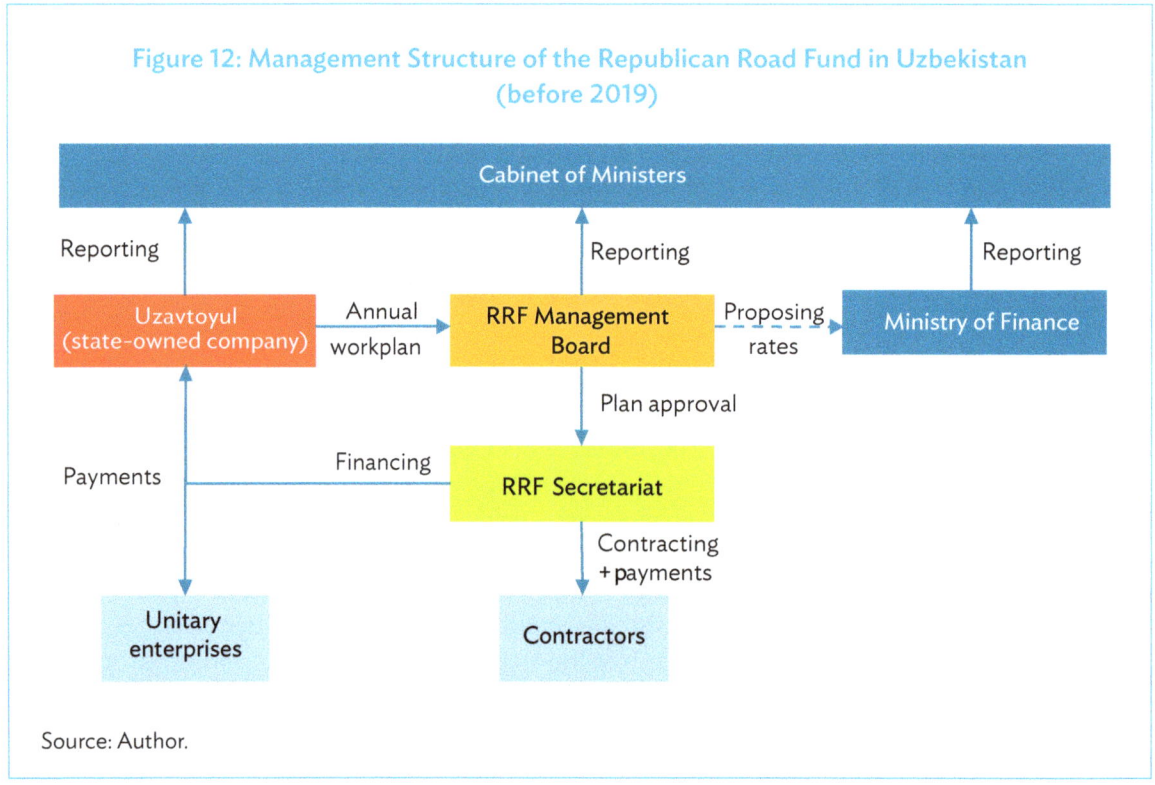

Figure 12: Management Structure of the Republican Road Fund in Uzbekistan (before 2019)

Source: Author.

With the abolishment of RRF and the creation of the Republican Fund in 2019, the fund was placed under the Ministry of Finance again. It is no longer a legal entity and is set up as a simple treasury account managed by a new Department for the Management of Funds for Road Development under the Ministry of Finance, involving a team of 10 people. This department is responsible for forecasting revenues and expenditures, reviewing annual work plans and cost estimates submitted by the Committee for Roads, distribution of transfer funds among the different regional funds, and preparing quarterly and annual implementation reports. As such, it functions as the secretariat of the Republican Fund. The regional funds are similarly placed under the Ministry of Finance of the Republic of Karakalpakstan and the finance departments of the regional governments and the city of Tashkent, with management by a newly created Sectors for the Management of Funds for Road Development. The Republic Fund and regional funds do not have any management boards, and approval of annual work plans is by the Cabinet of Ministers.

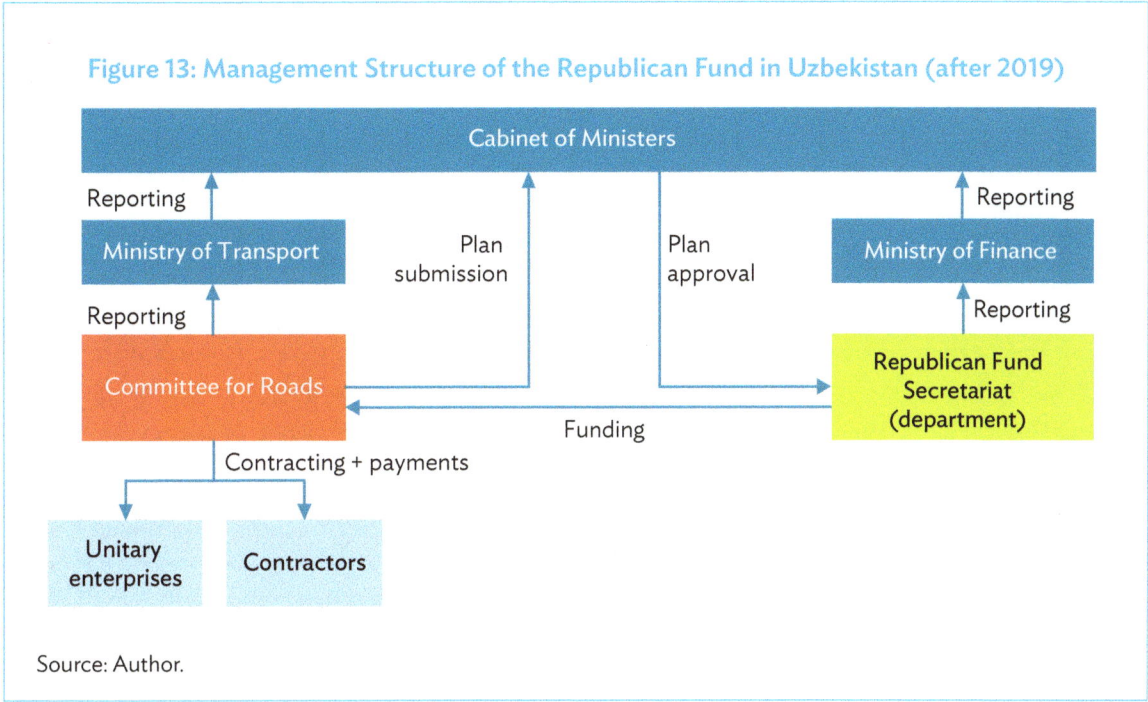

Figure 13: Management Structure of the Republican Fund in Uzbekistan (after 2019)

Source: Author.

Funding Approval and Allocation

The preparation of the annual works program to be financed by RRF used to be the responsibility of *Uzavtoyul*. Construction and reconstruction works had to be included in the investment program of the government before they could be financed by the RRF, and all project documentation had to be complete. For capital repairs (rehabilitation) works, approved designs and cost estimates for individual projects were required. Implementation of capital repairs was initially reserved for the construction enterprises under *Uzavtoyul*, which would compete with each other for the contracts. For maintenance and current repair (including periodic maintenance), *Uzavtoyul* only needed to provide cost estimates, with the work distributed among the different maintenance enterprises under *Uzavtoyul*.

After approval of the annual budget, the approved funding was transferred to *Uzavtoyul*, which in turn transferred the implementation funds to its subordinate entities. The Directorate for the Construction and Reconstruction of Public Roads was responsible for contracting the construction and reconstruction works through open competitive bidding. The Regional Road Departments under *Uzavtoyul* were responsible for coordinating the maintenance and repair. Capital repair works were contracted out through competitive bidding that was restricted to the construction enterprises under *Uzavtoyul* (for smaller contracts of less than $25,000, the works were distributed among the construction enterprises). This was later changed to full competitive bidding when the construction enterprises were corporatized and privatized. In the case of road maintenance and current repair, the works were distributed to the individual road maintenance enterprises under *Uzavtoyul*.

The 2006 Decree #499 updated the regulations of RRF and made RRF responsible for preparing the annual work program together with *Uzavtoyul*. RRF also became responsible for preparing the feasibility studies and other documentation for construction and reconstruction projects. RRF was further identified as the client for (re)construction, capital repair, and midterm repair works in international and national roads, making it responsible for tendering out (re)construction and capital or midterm repair works, and for carrying out the technical supervision for these works. The responsibility for maintenance and current repair remained with *Uzavtoyul*. With the merger of current repairs and midterm repairs in 2011, the implementation of midterm repairs (periodic maintenance) became the responsibility of *Uzavtoyul* again. In 2017, the State Committee for Roads became the client for (re)construction and repair works in public roads in the case of domestic funding, and RRF was only responsible for managing projects funded by development partners.

The year 2019 saw significant institutional reform with the abolishment of the RRF and the creation of the MOT and the underlying Committee for Roads. Decree #5890 of the same year introduced further reform, making the new Committee for Roads the sole client for all design, (re)construction, repair, and maintenance works. Development partner projects are managed by *Avtoyulinvest* under the Committee for Roads.

Detailed annual work plans for design and (re)construction of public roads are prepared by the Committee for Roads and submitted to the Ministry of Economy and Industry for inclusion in the Program for Development of Social and Industrial Infrastructure. Together with the plans for maintenance and repairs prepared by the Committee for Roads, the annual work plan is then submitted to the Cabinet of Ministers for approval. The approved plan is subsequently submitted to the Ministry of Finance as a budget request for financing from the Republican Fund. The Ministry of Finance reviews the budget request and compares this against expected revenues of the fund, including the final plan as part of the state budget for the following year.

Once the budget has been approved, funds are transferred to the treasury accounts of the SUE Directorate for Construction and Reconstruction of Public Roads for the design, (re)construction, and capital repair of public roads; the Committee for Roads and its Regional Road Departments for the maintenance and current repair of public roads; the Committee for Roads and its subordinate maintenance enterprises for the procurement of approved equipment; certain specialized enterprises for the maintenance and current repair of specific road sections; the SUE Customer Service for Regional Roads for the design, (re)construction, and repair of urban and rural roads; Tashkent City Government for the design, (re)construction, and capital repair of urban streets in Tashkent; and to other organizations acting as client for certain roadworks.

Financial and Technical Accountability

The 1993 road funds were simple treasury accounts managed directly by the entities responsible for the different roads. In 2003, the RRF was set up as a separate legal entity under the Ministry of Finance, with treasury accounts, accounts in commercial banks, and a special purpose foreign currency account in the Central Bank of Uzbekistan. Revenues and expenditures of the RRF were included in the annual state budget as targeted funds, and were included in the balance sheet of RRF. Unused funds remained with the RRF and were carried over to the next financial year. The RRF was allowed to place funds that were not directly needed in commercial bank accounts or even foreign bank accounts to collect interest.

The RRF was also able to receive international and foreign funding for investment projects. As such it had a large responsibility in financial management of the earmarked revenues.

The 2003 RRF regulations required that the Executive Directorate prepare monthly accounting reports and submit these to the Ministry of Finance after approval by the RRF Management Board. Control of the use of funding was the responsibility of the Ministry of Finance. Control over revenues was the responsibility of the State Tax Committee, the State Customs Committee, and the Ministry of Internal Affairs that were responsible for collection of the earmarked RRF revenues and were required to submit monthly reports to RRF on collected revenues. *Uzavtoyul* and later the State Committee for Roads were required to submit monthly, quarterly, and annual reports on the use of RRF funds. RRF regulations allowed it to carry out audits and inspections of works carried out by *Uzavtoyul* and the State Committee for Roads and their maintenance and current repair enterprises and other subordinate entities. The 2017 Resolution #361 requires the Main Control and Auditing Department of the Ministry of Finance to carry out annual audits of the RRF together with the State Tax Committee.

After abolishment of the RRF, the 2019 regulations for the new Republican Fund define that the Ministry of Finance, through its Department for the Management of Funds for Road Development, is responsible for maintaining accounts on revenues and expenditures. Client organizations must report on a monthly basis on the use of funding from the Republican Fund, including the work carried out using this funding. Information on revenues and expenditures is to be discussed with the general public and the relevant ministries, and published in media and websites. These regulations contain only limited detail on the accounting and reporting procedures for the new Republican Fund.

Road Fund Revenue

Uzbekistan has long had a history of earmarked charges that provide revenues to the road funds. This initially involved a corporate turnover tax, but also included specific road user charges. In the years after the abolishment of the RRF in 2019, the main road user charges related to the RRF were themselves also abolished. The current Republican Fund does not have earmarked road user charges and is dependent on annual budget allocations. Contrary to the Republican Fund, the regional funds do have earmarked road user charges that are collected at regional or district level. The lack of adequate earmarked funding is jeopardizing the financing of adequate road maintenance and repair of public roads. There are road user charges that are already being collected in Uzbekistan, and that provide adequate amounts of funding, but currently these are not earmarked for the Republican Fund or regional funds.

Revenue Sources

With the establishment of the RRF in 2003, the same sources of funding were applied that existed for the 1993 republican, regional, and local road funds. The most important of these was a corporate turnover tax that was paid by companies. This was a common source of funding for early road funds in former Soviet countries, even though it cannot be considered to be a road user charge. This was complemented by a vehicle registration fee and a foreign vehicle entry fee, which became more important over time. Although the RRF regulations also mention a fuel tax in the Republic of Karakalpakstan, this was never allocated to the RRF.

Table 40: Sources of Funding of the Republican Road Fund

- Corporate turnover tax
- Vehicle registration fee
- Foreign vehicle entry fee
- Fuel tax in the Republic of Karakalpakstan
- Foreign loans, grants, and donations

Source: Republic Road Fund regulations, 2003.

With the abolishment of the RRF in 2019, the earmarking of these revenue sources also ended. The new Republican Fund no longer has earmarked road user charges, and instead depends on annual budget allocations. In the case of (re)construction and capital repair, funding comes from annual allocations from the state budget and interest-free loans from the Fund for Reconstruction and Development ($50 million in 2020, and $100 million per year for the period 2021–2024). In the case of maintenance and current repair (including periodic maintenance), allocations are to be provided from the budgets of the Republic of Karakalpakstan, the 12 regions, and the capital city Tashkent.

In the case of the 14 regional funds that are managed by the regional governments, funding should come from regional and local budget allocations, as well as from a regional fuel levy (up to a maximum rate of SUM25 per liter), parking fees, fees for technical inspections of vehicles, fees for roadside advertising, and 60% of fees for roadside structures and facilities within the right-of-way. These fees are all set by the regional governments and collected at the regional level. The regional funds may also receive transfers from the Republican Fund, but these may not be used for the maintenance and current repair of public roads, which is to be financed from regional budget allocations. Resolution #123 also introduces a vehicle ownership fee, but this goes directly to the city and district authorities for financing (re)construction and repair works in those cities and districts, and does not go through the regional funds.

This setup introduces a strange situation, where regional governments are expected to provide budget allocations to the Republican Fund to finance the maintenance and current repair of public roads that are the responsibility of the republican government. At the same time, the regional governments have to provide funding to the regional funds for the maintenance and current repair of rural and urban roads under their responsibility, while funding for the (re)construction and capital repair of these roads is provided from republican government allocations through transfers from the Republican Fund.

This is further complicated by the existence of the Fund for the Development and Support of the Activities of the Committee for Roads (Fund for the Committee for Roads) that finances operational costs and financial incentives for the Committee for Roads and its subordinate enterprises. This fund is financed from the foreign vehicle entry fee that used to finance the RRF. Of this revenue source, 80% goes to the fund, and the other 20% goes to the state budget. The Fund for the Committee for Roads is also financed from the remainder of the fee for structures and facilities in the right-of-way (40%).

Table 41: Sources of Funding of the Republican and Regional Trust Funds for Road Development

Republican Fund	Regional Funds	Fund for the Committee for Roads
• State budget allocations (construction and capital repair) • Interest-free loans from the Fund for Reconstruction and Development (construction and capital repair) • Regional budget allocations (maintenance and current repair)	• Fuel levies applied at regional level • Parking fees • Fees for technical inspections of vehicles • Fees for roadside advertising • Fees for roadside facilities (60%)	• Foreign vehicle entry fee (80%) • Fees for roadside facilities (40%)

Sources: 2003 Republican Road Fund regulations, and 2019 Resolution #4545.

Corporate turnover tax. The most important revenue source earmarked for the RRF was a corporate turnover tax applied to enterprises, farms, and organizations (1.5%); procurement, intermediary and trade enterprises (1.0%); banks, insurance companies, auctions, casinos, and events and video salons (1.5%); and motor transport enterprises (2.5%). The distinguished categories of enterprises and the tax percentages were adjusted in subsequent years, with tax payments collected by the State Tax Committee. The state budget for 2012 replaced the corporate turnover tax with a single compulsory contribution to state trust funds, combining it with other compulsory contributions. This single compulsory contribution for state trust funds had a tax rate of 3.5% of turnover, which was shared between the Pension Fund (1.6%); the RRF (1.4%); and the Fund for Reconstruction, Overhaul and Equipment of Educational and Medical Institutions (0.5%). This compulsory contribution to state trust funds was abolished in January 2019 through Presidential Decree #5468 together with the abolishment of the RRF.

Vehicle registration fee. Resolution #334 of 1993 earmarked a fee on the purchase and/or temporary import of vehicles into Uzbekistan, which was collected by the Ministry of Internal Affairs upon the registration of the vehicle. The fee was set at 6% of the sales value in the case of passenger cars, and 20% in the case of trucks, buses, and special vehicles. The fee structure was further amended in following years and, in 2016, the fees were set at 3% of the sales value for new vehicles, while for used vehicles the fee was set at a percentage of the minimum wage multiplied by the amount of horsepower of the vehicle, whereby the percentage depended on the type of vehicle and its age as presented in Table 42. With the abolishment of the RRF in 2019, this road user charge was initially transferred to the state budget, but since 2020 it was allocated to the regional budgets. In 2022, the government decided to abolish this road user charge completely.

Table 42: Vehicle Registration Fee for Used Vehicles
(% of minimum wage for each horsepower)

Vehicle Type	Less Than 3 Years Old	3–7 Years Old	More Than 7 Years Old
Motorcycle	10%	7%	5%
Passenger car	11%	9%	6%
Other vehicles	16%	13%	9%

Source: Law on the State Budget 2021 ZRU-589, 2020.

Foreign vehicle entry fee. Resolution #334 of 1993 also introduced a fee for the entry and transit of foreign vehicles into Uzbekistan, set at $400 per vehicle. Initially, this included both freight vehicles and buses, but later it was amended to only include freight vehicles. Over time, bilateral agreements and different rates were introduced with various countries. In addition to the foreign vehicle entry rates, additional fees may be charged for overweight or oversized vehicles as listed in the 1995 Resolution #11. The foreign vehicle entry fee used to be earmarked specifically for the road sector, with all revenue going to the RRF. With the abolishment of the RRF in 2019, 80% of the revenue now goes to the Fund for Development and Support of the Committee for Roads that serves to cover the operational costs of the Committee for Roads and its underlying departments and enterprises (this does not cover the costs of works), with the remaining 20% going to the state budget. The foreign vehicle entry fees are collected by the State Customs Committee. Rates are fixed in US dollars, but are collected in sum. This means that it is not a source of foreign currency as it could potentially be if payments were made in US dollars.

Table 43: Foreign Vehicle Entry Fees
(US$ per vehicle)

Country of Origin	Under 10 Tons	10–20 Tons	Over 20 Tons
Afghanistan[1]	$50	$50	$50
Azerbaijan	$100	$150	$200
Tajikistan	$100	$150	$200
Kazakhstan	$300	$300	$300
Kyrgyz Republic	$300	$300	$300
Turkmenistan	$50	$100	$150
European Union	$150	$150	$150
Other countries	$400	$400	$400

[1] ADB placed on hold its assistance in Afghanistan effective 15 August 2021. *ADB Statement on Afghanistan | Asian Development Bank* (published on 10 November 2021). Manila.
Source: Law on the State Budget 2022 ZRU-742, 2021.

Vehicle customs duty (not earmarked). The vehicle customs duty is collected when importing a vehicle. The rates are defined in the annual state budget and depend mainly on the type of vehicle and its engine capacity (in cubic centimeter). The 2019 state budget sets the following rates in US dollars. The additional rate that depends on the engine capacity, by far, is the most important, easily totaling a few thousand dollars. The vehicle customs duty is collected by the State Customs Committee. This revenue is not earmarked for any road fund.

Fuel consumption excise tax (not earmarked). The state budget for 2002 introduced a tax from individuals on the consumption of petrol, diesel, and gas for vehicles (consumption tax), replacing the ownership tax from individuals paid on vehicles. The rate was set at SUM20 per liter for petrol and diesel, and SUM17 per kilogram for compressed gas. This consumption tax was applied to the end user at the petrol stations, and the tax reporting was carried out by the petrol stations on a monthly basis. Revenue was collected by the State Tax Committee and was fully transferred to the budgets of the Republic of

Karakalpakstan, the regional governments, and the city of Tashkent. In 2011, liquefied gas was included with a tax rate applied per liter, while for compressed gas the rate was applied per cubic meter. By 2018, the rate had increased to SUM233 per liter for petrol and diesel, SUM230 per liter for liquefied gas, and SUM305 per cubic meter for compressed gas.

Table 44: Vehicle Customs Duty for 2019
(US$)

Vehicle Type	Base Rate	Additional Rate
Motorcycle	20	
Passenger car	30–40	2.0–3.0 per cm³
Bus (≥10 passengers)	20	2.0 per cm³
Freight vehicle (<5 tons)	30	1.2 per cm³
Freight vehicle (5–20 tons)	70	1.2 per cm³
Freight vehicle (>20 tons)	70	3.0 per cm³
(Semi-)trailers	5	
Tanker and self-loading (semi-)trailers	15	

cm³ = cubic centimeter.
Source: Presidential Resolution #4086 for the 2019 State Budget.

In 2019, the fuel consumption tax was replaced by a fuel excise tax for end consumers through an amendment to the Tax Code (ZRU-508, December 2018). The rates of the fuel consumption excise tax have continued to increase, reaching SUM385 ($0.04) per liter for petrol, diesel, and liquefied gas, and SUM550 ($0.05) per cubic meter for compressed natural gas in 2022. With the change to an excise tax, the tax is no longer collected by the petrol stations, but is applied directly to the retail price set by the government and collected by the State Tax Committee. The revenue from this fuel excise tax for end consumers continues to be transferred to the Republic of Karakalpakstan, the regions, and the city of Tashkent according to the fuel consumption in these areas. This revenue is not earmarked for any road fund.

Table 45: Fuel Consumption Excise Tax
(SUM/liter or SUM/cubic meter)

Fuel Type	2013	2014	2015	2016	2017	2018	2019	2020	2021	2022
Gasoline	240/l	265/l	290/l	335/l	465/l	233/l	285/l	285/l	350/l	385/l
Diesel	240/l	265/l	290/l	335/l	465/l	233/l	285/l	285/l	350/l	385/l
Liquefied gas	165/l	180/l	200/l	230/l	230/l	230/l	285/l	285/l	350/l	385/l
Natural gas	200/m³	220/m³	240/m³	275/m³	275/m³	305/m³	435/m³	435/m³	500/m³	550/m³

l = liter, m³ = cubic meter.
Sources: State budgets for the years concerned, and Tax Code 2020.

Fuel production excise tax (not earmarked). Apart from the fuel excise tax to end users that replaced the fuel consumption tax, the government also applies a fuel excise tax to the fuel produced in Uzbekistan or imported into the country. This was originally an ad valorem tax equivalent to a percentage of the wholesale price. From 2008 onward, the ad valorem rates were changed to fixed rates for petrol and diesel, while ad valorem percentages continue to be used for compressed natural gas and liquefied gas. The rates used to be set in the state budget, but are now set in the Tax Code. The rates for the different fuel types for the last 10 years are listed in Table 46. This revenue is not earmarked for any road fund.

Table 46: Fuel Excise Tax
(SUM per ton, %)

Fuel Type	2013	2014	2015	2016	2017	2018	2019	2020	2021	2022
Petrol A-72, A-76, A-80	321,430	321,430	321,430	321,430	321,430	321,430	200,000	200,000	240,000	275,000
Petrol A-91, A-92, A-93	353,430	353,430	353,430	353,430	353,430	353,430	250,000	250,000	275,000	275,000
Petrol A-95	408,890	408,890	408,890	408,890	408,890	408,890	250,000	250,000	275,000	275,000
Diesel	273,400	273,400	273,400	273,400	273,400	273,400	200,000	200,000	240,000	264,000
Diesel ECO	284,250	284,250	284,250	284,250	284,250	284,250	180,000	180,000	216,000	237,600
Engine oil	207,000	207,000	207,000	207,000	207,000	207,000	250,000	250,000	340,000	374,000
Natural gas	25%	25%	25%	25%	25%	15%	20%	20%	20%	20%
Liquefied gas	26%	26%	26%	26%	26%	26%	30%	30%	30%	-

Sources: State budget and Budget Code.

Tolling (not earmarked). Tolls are not yet collected on roads in Uzbekistan. The 2007 Law on Roads expressly mentions that road tolling is to be dealt with in a separate law. The 2019 draft Strategy for Development of the Transport System until 2035 speaks of the need to develop a law on toll roads and related procedures as the basis for introducing tolling in high-speed roads. These toll roads would be constructed through PPP as alternative routes to existing roads. Decree #5890 of 2019 speaks of the construction of high-speed toll roads, with Resolution #4545 identifying a set of five road and tunnel projects that are considered suitable for tolling under PPPs. These include Tashkent-Andijan, Tashkent-Samarkand, Syrdarya-Bakht, Kamchik Pass tunnel, and Takhtakarachi Pass tunnel. Of these, feasibility studies are currently being prepared for Tashkent-Andijan and Tashkent-Samarkand.

A draft Law on Toll Roads was prepared in August 2019. This focuses on the creation of new expressway routes that are operated as toll roads under PPPs. Financing may come from the government or from private partners. The draft law requires that there be an alternative route that is not tolled. The tolling policy and maximum toll rates are to be set by the Cabinet of Ministers, while the Committee for Roads would be responsible for ensuring compliance with the norms and standards and the contract agreement, including the quality of construction, repair, and maintenance works. Where part of the toll revenue goes to the government, this is to be reserved for road sector development.

Road tolling appears only to be considered for the construction of new high-speed roads under PPPs. Initial assessments indicate that tolling will likely be insufficient to cover the full costs of construction and maintenance under traditional build–operate–transfer arrangements and would need to be complemented by availability payments. Alternatively, the use of government or development partner funding could be provided to finance the initial construction, with road tolling and PPP arrangements focusing on the subsequent operation and maintenance. Applying tolling on existing roads is currently not being considered as a means of financing the operation and maintenance of these roads.

Revenue Levels

Although the corporate turnover tax and the subsequent compulsory contribution to state trust funds, strictly speaking, are not road user charges, they formed the most important source of funding for the RRF, providing an average of $500 million per year between 2013 and 2017 and forming 55%–70% of total RRF funding and 70%–80% of earmarked revenues. Although revenue in Uzbekistan sum continued to increase, the devaluation following the liberalization of the sum in September 2017 resulted in the 2018 revenue dropping to $335 million.

Revenues from the vehicle registration fee quadrupled between 2013 and 2018 in Uzbekistan sum terms, but remained relatively steady in US dollar terms, providing an average $150 million per year. For the foreign vehicle entry fees, revenues in Uzbekistan sum terms tripled in the period 2013–2018, but in US dollar terms it remained relatively steady, averaging just under $20 million per year. Additional funding came from development partners and other income sources, including state budget allocations. Total revenue of the RRF averaged about $1,000 million per year, dropping to $650 million in 2018 as a result of the devaluation of the sum. Available RRF budgets were generally not fully utilized, with significant balances carried over from one year to the next. The revenues of the RRF are presented in Table 47 in Uzbekistan sum, and in Figure 14 in US dollars.

Table 47: Annual Revenues of the Republican Road Fund 2013–2018
(SUM billion)

Revenue Source	2013	2014	2015	2016	2017	2018
Corporate turnover tax	1,090	1,298	1,206	1,431	1,866	2,630
Vehicle registration fee	252	364	463	463	612	1,044
Foreign vehicle entry fee	44	47	41	42	83	154
Development partner loans	128	332	490	529	326	463
Other income	28	70	65	58	521	30
Subtotal	**1,542**	**2,112**	**2,265**	**2,523**	**3,408**	**4,322**
Balance from previous year	653	296	342	418	413	724
Total (SUM billion)	**2,195**	**2,407**	**2,607**	**2,941**	**3,821**	**5,046**
Exchange rate: US$1	2,093	2,305	2,531	2,933	3,942	7,850
Total (US$ million)	**$1,049**	**$1,044**	**$1,030**	**$1,003**	**$969**	**$643**

Source: Republican Road Fund.

Since the establishment of the new Republican Fund in 2019, financing for the road sector initially came through state budget allocations to the MOT. Only in the 2022 budget was funding specifically allocated through the Republican Fund. The MOT budget averaged SUM5,836 billion ($562 million) in 2020 and 2021, although this also included budget allocations for other transport sectors. The allocation from the Republican Fund in 2022 amounted to SUM4,820 billion ($445 million), significantly lower than the $643 million of the RRF in 2018 and much lower than the average RRF budget level of $1,000 per year for the years before the devaluation of the Uzbekistan sum.

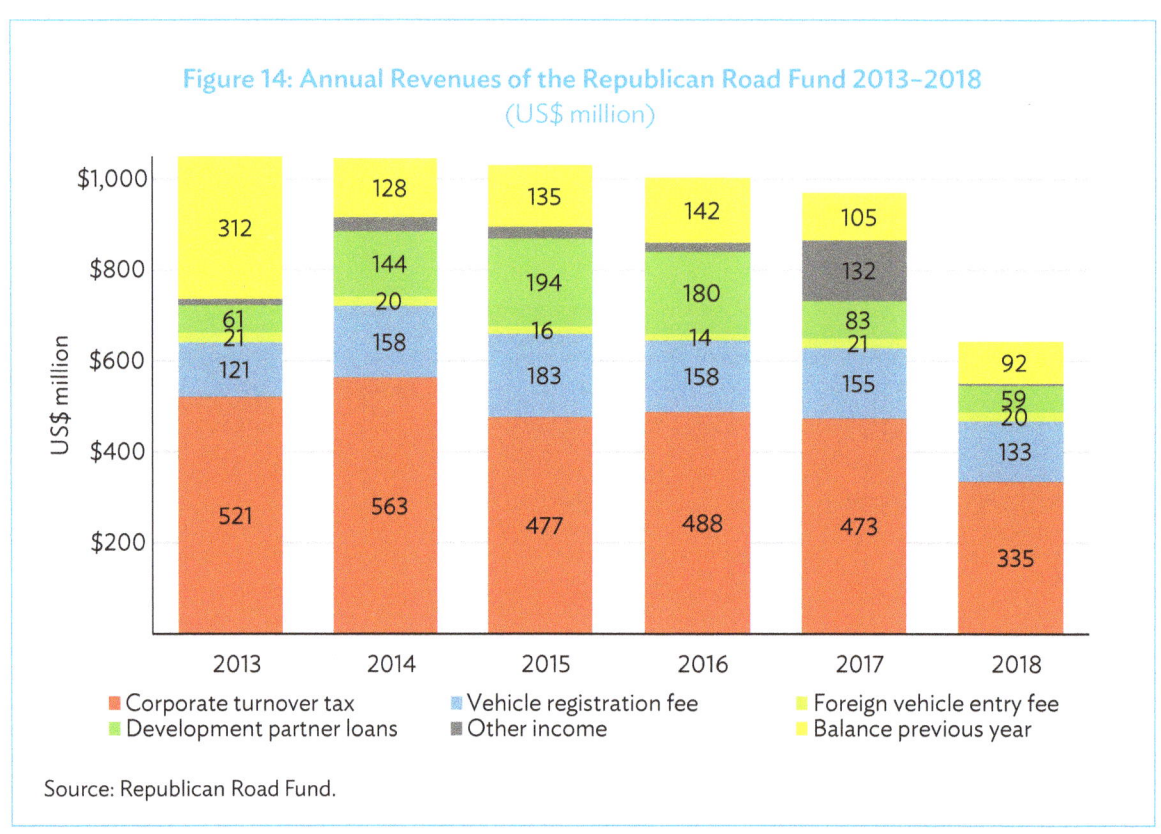

Figure 14: Annual Revenues of the Republican Road Fund 2013–2018 (US$ million)

Source: Republican Road Fund.

Table 48: Annual Budgets of the Ministry of Transport (SUM billion)

Budget Line	2020	2021	2022
Current expenses	1,899	3,439	177
Capital investments	2,961	3,373	880
Transfer from Republican Trust Fund for Road Development	–	–	4,820
Total (SUM billion)	**4,860**	**6,812**	**5,877**
Exchange rate: US$1	10,143	10,550	10,840
Total (US$ million)	$479.2	$645.6	$542.2

Sources: State budgets 2020, 2021, and 2022.

Fuel excise taxes (not earmarked). Based on the fuel consumption for road transport as reported by the State Statistical Committee, the revenue from the fuel consumption and fuel production excise taxes related to road transport can be estimated. Table 49 shows the 2020 fuel consumption for road transport in tons, and the estimated revenue from the fuel production and fuel consumption excise taxes calculated by multiplying the consumption by the 2020 excise tax rates (note that these are significantly lower than the 2022 rates). The 2020 revenue from the fuel production excise tax is estimated to be in the order of $150 million, while for the fuel consumption excise tax the revenue is estimated to be in the order of $200 million. These revenues are separate from the fuel levies applied at the regional level. Although these are important road user charges with significant revenues, they are not earmarked as sources of funding for the road sector, nor have they been at any time in their existence. The fuel production excise tax is currently allocated to the state budget and, in the future, may be allocated to the Republican Fund. The fuel consumption excise tax is currently allocated to the regional government budgets and, therefore, it will be harder to earmark this to the Republican Fund, although it could be considered for earmarking to the regional funds.

Table 49: Estimated Fuel Production Excise Tax Revenue (2020)

Fuel Type	Production (tons)	Excise Rate[a] (SUM/ton)	Revenue (SUM billion)	Revenue (US$ million)
Petrol	1,244,000	233,333	290.3	$28.62
Diesel	1,244,700	190,000	236.5	$23.32
Liquefied gas	382,200	280,000	107.0	$10.55
Natural gas	2,541,100	350,000	889.4	$87.68
Total			**1,523.2**	**$150.17**

[a] For liquefied and natural gas, estimations were used since the tax is defined as a percentage of the wholesale price.
Sources: State Statistics Committee (https://stat.uz), and Tax Code 2020.

Table 50: Estimated Fuel Consumption Excise Tax Revenue (2020)

Fuel Type	Production (ton)	Excise Rate (SUM/ton)	Revenue (SUM billion)	Revenue (US$ million)
Petrol	1,244,000	378,480	470.8	$46.42
Diesel	1,244,700	346,275	431.0	$42.49
Liquefied gas	382,200	540,645	206.6	$20.37
Natural gas	2,541,100	391,500	994.8	$98.08
Total			**2,103.3**	**$207.37**

Sources: State Statistics Committee (https://stat.uz), and Tax Code 2020.

Vehicle customs duty (not earmarked). Uzbekistan has about 60,000 new registrations of vehicles each year, including 13,900 commercial vehicles and 47,500 passenger cars in 2018.[11] However, the large majority of these vehicles are produced domestically through joint ventures between government and General Motors for passenger cars and MANN for trucks. As a result, the vehicle customs duty is not collected for these vehicles. The low number of imported vehicles for which the vehicle customs duty is collected, results in limited revenues from this road user charge. Revenue from the vehicle customs duty goes to the state budget and could relatively easily be earmarked for the Republican Fund.

Revenue Allocation

The expenditure of the RRF revenue is presented in Table 51 and Figure 15. The main portion of 41% is spent on (re)construction and capital repair of public roads, which includes funding provided by development partners for these projects (just over one-quarter of the total funding spent on these types of works). A further 34% is spent on maintenance and current repair, including the procurement of equipment for the road maintenance enterprises. Up until 2017, the allocations to the RRF secretariat, *Uzavtoyul,* and underlying entities averaged only 0.7% of the RRF budget. However, in 2017 *Uzavtoyul* was transformed into the State Committee for Roads, resulting in increasing allocations to the subordinate units and to the new State Inspectorate and the unitary enterprise Landscaping, with operational costs increasing to 3.4% in 2018.

Table 51: Expenditure of the Republican Road Fund
(SUM billion)

Expenditure Item	2013	2014	2015	2016	2017	2018
Design	11.5	5.8	11.7	7.8	9.1	13.7
Construction and capital repair	916.6	969.9	1,061.1	1,526.4	1,471.3	1,891.8
RRF	792.5	637.7	571.1	997.6	1,145.5	1,428.6
IFIs	124.1	332.2	490.0	528.8	325.8	463.2
Maintenance and current repair	658.4	647.9	754.9	808.7	1,055.7	1,821.8
Maintenance equipment	62.5	88.6	16.7	51.7	125.6	388.8
Emergency maintenance	29.8	48.9	49.0	30.5	67.0	83.0
Operational costs	11.8	14.1	19.6	24.1	41.3	180.8
RRF	3.5	4.4	5.1	5.9	5.1	2.5
Uzavtoyul/SCR	1.1	1.5	2.3	2.8	5.6	9.7
Regional Road Departments	7.2	8.2	12.2	15.4	27.5	134.5
UE Landscaping	0.0	0.0	0.0	0.0	0.0	27.3
State Inspectorate	0.0	0.0	0.0	0.0	3.1	6.8
Foreign vehicle entry fee collection	0.0	1.0	0.8	0.6	0.5	0.9

continued on next page

---

[11] Countryeconomy.com. Uzbekistan-new motor vehicle registrations. https://countryeconomy.com/business/car-registrations/uzbekistan.

Table 51 continued

Expenditure Item	2013	2014	2015	2016	2017	2018
Other expenditure	208.5	289.4	275.3	136.6	326.8	310.6
Subtotal	**1,899.1**	**2,065.7**	**2,189.0**	**2,586.5**	**3,097.2**	**4,691.3**
Balance at end of the year	295.6	341.7	418.0	354.1	724.2	354.9
Total (SUM billion)	**2,194.7**	**2,407.3**	**2,607.0**	**2,940.6**	**3,821.3**	**5,046.2**
Exchange rate: US$1	2,093	2,305	2,531	2,933	3,942	7,850
Total (US$ million)	**$1,048.6**	**$1,044.4**	**$1,030.0**	**$1,002.6**	**$968.7**	**$642.0**

IFI = international finance institution, RRF = Republic Road Fund, SCR = State Committee for Roads, UE = unitary enterprise.

Source: Republican Road Fund.

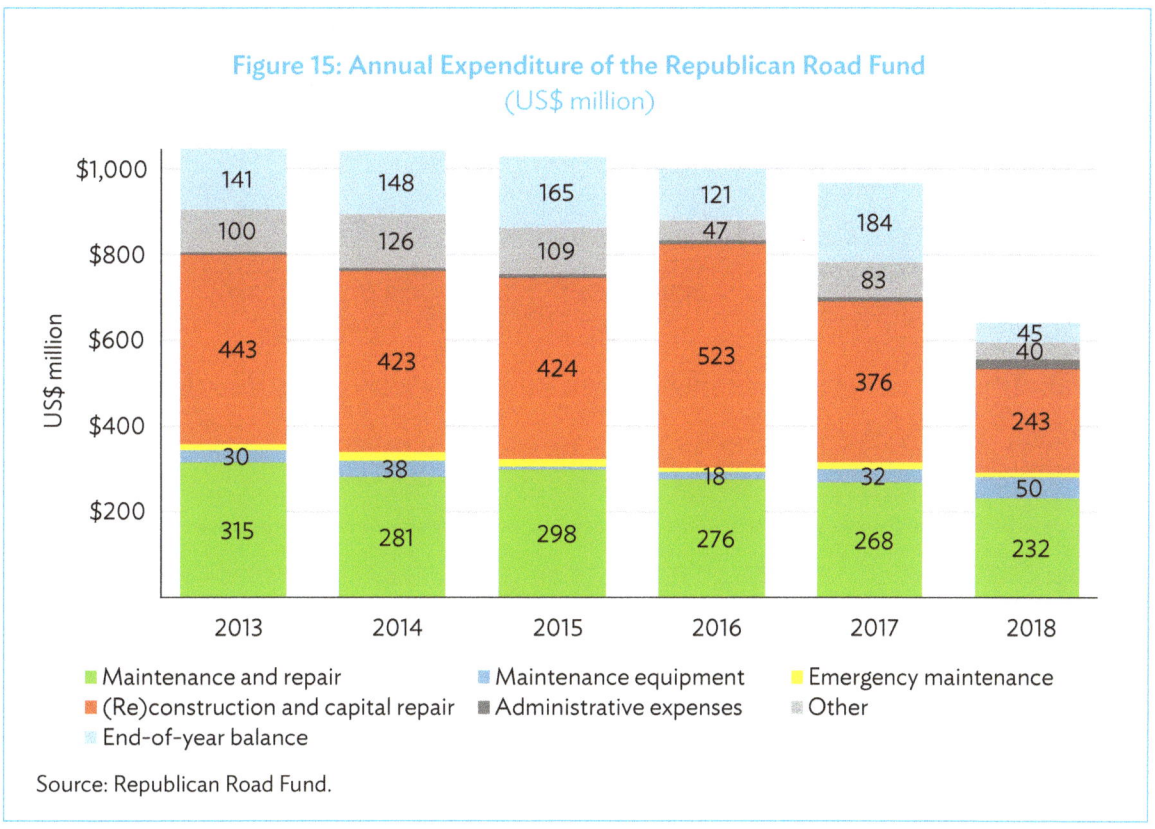

Figure 15: Annual Expenditure of the Republican Road Fund (US$ million)

Source: Republican Road Fund.

The expenditure of *Uzavtoyul* and the subsequent State Committee for Roads and Committee for Roads are presented in Table 52 in sum, and in Figure 16 in US dollars. Note that this goes beyond 2018 and includes 3 years after the abolishment of the RRF in which road sector funding came from annual budget allocations (formal transfers from the Republican Fund only started in 2022). Although expenditure in public roads remained more or less stable after 2018, this now also covers activities formerly carried out directly by RRF as can be seen by the increase in expenditure on construction and reconstruction, implying that actual expenditure has decreased compared to 2018. This is also reflected in a gradual decrease in funding allocated to maintenance and current repair in 2019 and 2020. In 2021, a significant increase in expenditure in public roads was achieved, especially in maintenance and current repair. However, as can be seen in Table 48, the available budget dropped in the following year. Table 52 and Figure 16 also include funding for the repair of regional (rural and urban) roads, which is carried out through the SUE Corporate Services under the Committee for Roads. This funding does not come through the MOT or from the Republican Fund. Currently, the government is putting a lot of emphasis on improving the large network of rural and urban roads, and this funding now makes up a major portion of the expenditure of the Committee for Roads.

Table 52: Expenditure by Uzavtoyul, State Committee for Roads, and Committee for Roads
(SUM billion)

Intervention Type	2014	2015	2016	2017	2018	2019	2020	2021
Construction/reconstruction	434	591	429	618	687	1,158	1,189	1,462
Capital repair (rehabilitation)	142	169	83	222	392	416	416	448
Current repair and maintenance	400	528	632	829	1,543	1,377	1,359	2,565
Subtotal	976	1,288	1,144	1,668	2,622	2,951	2,964	4,475
Repair of regional roads	120	100	164	368	910	1,283	1,221	2,857
Total (SUM billion)	1,095	1,387	1,308	2,036	3,531	4,234	4,185	7,332
Exchange rate: US$1	2,305	2,531	2,933	3,942	7,850	8,520	10,143	10,550
Total (US$ million)	$475.1	$548.1	$445.9	$516.6	$449.8	$496.9	$412.6	$695.0

Source: Committee for Roads website.

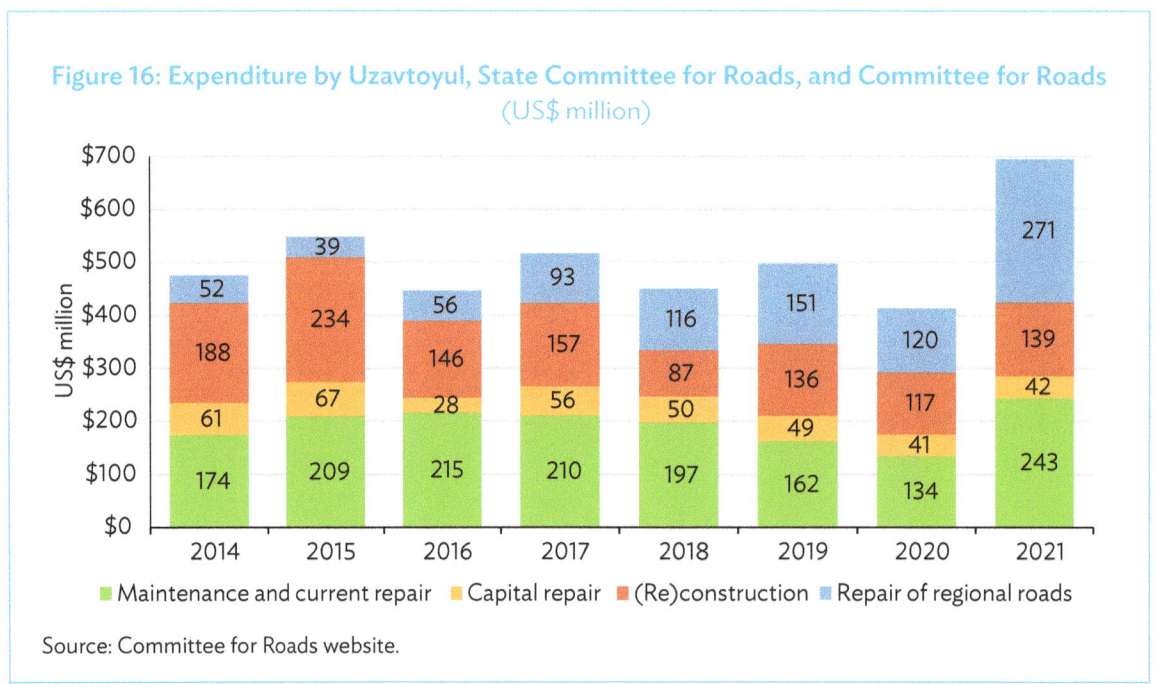

Figure 16: Expenditure by Uzavtoyul, State Committee for Roads, and Committee for Roads (US$ million)

Source: Committee for Roads website.

A closer look at the expenditure on maintenance and current repair shows how the expenditure on winter and summer maintenance has continued to increase, while expenditure on current repair (including periodic maintenance) decreased after 2018. The length of road covered by current repair has also decreased since 2018. At its highest point, current repair only covered 3,752 km of roads, equivalent to less than 1% of the public road length and only 20% of the length of international and national roads. By 2020, coverage dropped to only 12% of the international and national road network. Given the fact that current repairs include both small pavement repairs that are required every year as well as wearing course renewals that are required every few years, this level of coverage is well below what is necessary to avoid the accelerated deterioration of the roads and the need for costly capital repairs in the future. In US dollars, the expenditure per kilometer on current repair also shows a significant decrease over the years, dropping from $65,000/km in 2016 to only $30,000/km in 2020. This implies that wearing course renewals are forming a gradually decreasing portion of the works carried out under current repairs, with the focus shifting to isolated minor repairs.

Table 53: Expenditure on Current Repair and Maintenance
(SUM billion)

Intervention Type	2016	2017	2018	2019	2020
Winter maintenance	24	38	34	39	65
Landscaping	7	10	109	85	99
Summer maintenance	182	222	388	353	484
Current repair	402	558	1,059	746	673
(length of works carried out)	(2,100 km)	(2,850 km)	(3,752 km)	(2,350 km)	(2,270 km)
Total	**615**	**828**	**1,590**	**1,224**	**1,321**

km = kilometer.
Source: Data provided by Committee for Roads.

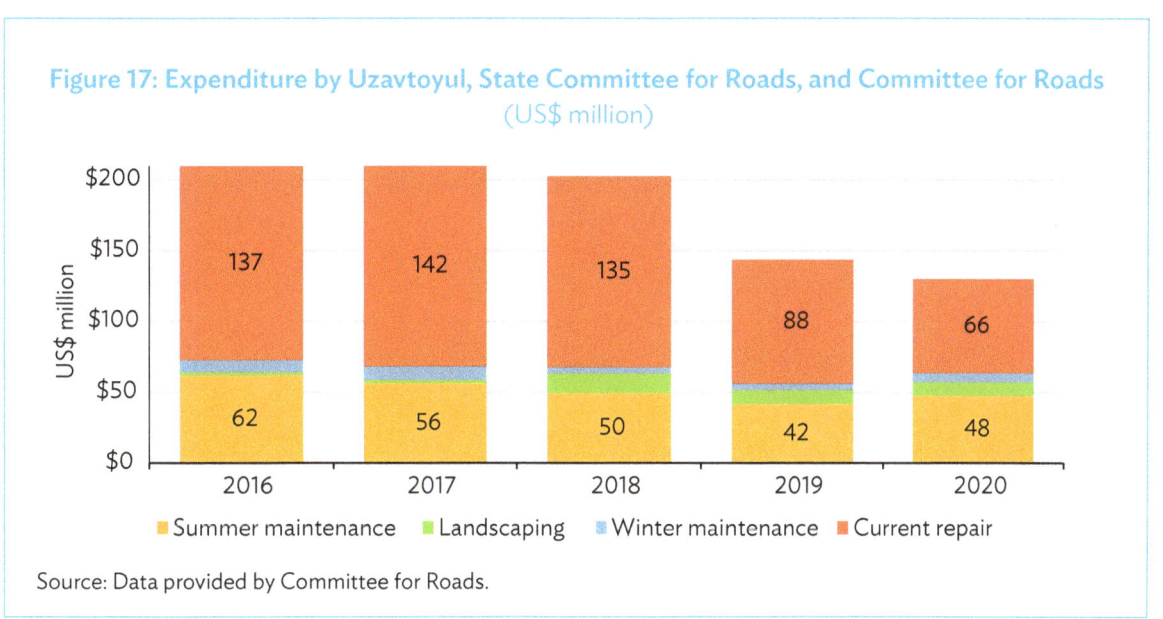

Figure 17: Expenditure by Uzavtoyul, State Committee for Roads, and Committee for Roads
(US$ million)

Source: Data provided by Committee for Roads.

In 2022, the first formal allocation from the Republican Fund was reflected in the budget. According to the budget allocations, 50% of the available budget from the Republican Fund is allocated to (re)construction of public roads and procurement of equipment in accordance with the Program for Development of Social and Industrial Infrastructure, reflecting an increase in funding compared to 2018 and a similar level of funding as 2021. Most of the other half of the allocated funding (44%) is allocated to maintenance, current repair, and capital repair of public roads. This reflects a significant decrease in funding for maintenance and repair, both compared to the RRF funding in 2018 and the budget allocations in 2021. Allocations to the Committee for Roads and subordinate entities have gone back down to 2017 levels, reflecting the fact that all costs of the road maintenance enterprises are now covered by the awarded contracts (and thus included in the maintenance and repair budget) and that operational expenses of the Committee for Roads are covered separately under the Fund for the Development and Support of the Activities of the Committee for Roads.

Table 54: Budget Allocations from the Republican Fund in 2022
(SUM billion)

Budget Item	Budget	Percentage
Construction, reconstruction, and equipment procurement	2,400	50%
Maintenance, current and capital repair	2,135	44%
Emergency repair	232	5%
Committee for Roads and subordinate entities	53	1%
Total	**4,820**	**100%**

Source: State budget 2022.

Funding Needs

An HDM4 analysis was carried out in 2014 under the CAREC Corridor 2 Road Investment Program. Initially, the analysis focused on the international road network, determining that an optimal budget of $146 million per year was required for the first 5 years to address the maintenance and repair backlog, about evenly distributed between midterm repair (periodic maintenance) and capital repair (rehabilitation), with a smaller allocation to maintenance and current repair. Lower budgets of down to $85 million per year would still lead to a stabilization of the international road network, but would not allow an improvement of average conditions. After addressing the initial backlog, budget requirements could be reduced to $64 million per year.

The analysis was later expanded to also include national and local roads, covering the entire public road network. The optimal budget allocation was determined to be $913 million per year for the first 5 years, and $433 million per year after the backlog had been addressed, giving a total requirement of $11,054 million for the 20-year analysis period. A minimum budget of $580 million per year was considered necessary for the first 5 years to stabilize the network, but this would lead to higher costs in subsequent years. These cost estimates do not include the maintenance and repair costs for bridges and other structures.

A basic analysis carried out as part of the preparation of the Road Subsector Development Strategy in 2021 came to a similar estimation of funding needs. This analysis was based on unit costs and average frequencies of different treatments for different road standards. It estimated that an annual budget was required of $370 million per year, including $280 million per year for midterm repair (periodic maintenance), $35 million per year for current repair (routine pavement maintenance), $27 million per year for off-carriageway routine maintenance, and $27 million per year for winter maintenance. This cost estimation does not include capital repair needs. This compared well to the analysis of the Committee for Roads, which estimated that $350 million was required each year to cover maintenance and current repair (including periodic maintenance).

The estimated funding needs of $350 million–$400 million per year for maintenance and current repair (including periodic maintenance) are about double the 2018 RRF allocations and triple the 2020 budget allocations. Although the 2021 allocations for maintenance and current repair reached $240 million, the 2022 budget allocation dropped back to $200 million, including capital repairs (implying significantly lower allocations to maintenance and current repair). To a large extent, this is because of the fact that the Republican Fund does not have any earmarked funding for maintenance and repair, and is dependent on budget allocations from regional governments. With the current focus on improving rural and urban roads, it is unlikely that these allocations from regional governments will increase very much in future years.

At the same time, there are other road user charges that are currently being collected, but that are not earmarked for the Republican Fund or regional funds. The most important of these are the fuel production excise tax and the fuel consumption excise tax (previously collected at fuel stations but now collected at wholesale level). These two road user charges together provide a revenue in the order of $350 million per year. Assuming that it may not be possible to earmark the fuel consumption excise tax to the Republican Fund since it is currently allocated to the regional budgets, this would still leave the fuel production excise tax that provides about $150 million in revenues. This would allow a significant portion of the funding needs for maintenance and current repair (including periodic maintenance) of public roads to be covered. The fuel consumption excise tax may be earmarked for the regional funds, allowing maintenance and current repair and possibly even some capital repair of rural and urban roads to be financed.

ROAD FUND MANAGEMENT

This chapter summarizes the experiences in the five countries with regard to the management of their road funds, identifying lessons and best practices and providing recommendations for further strengthening of road fund management in these countries, as well as other countries in the CAREC region and beyond. In particular, it looks at the eligible activities funded by the road funds, the management structure applied, the procedures for annual work plan preparation and approval, and the financial and technical accountability regarding the use of road fund financing.

Eligible Activities

The activities that are financed from the road fund vary from country to country. Although all reviewed road funds finance maintenance and repair, some road funds go further and also finance construction and reconstruction of roads and the procurement of equipment for underlying state-owned maintenance entities. In some cases, certain activities receive priority in the allocation of funds, or limitations are defined regarding the percentage of road fund financing that can be allocated to specific activities. An overview of the eligible activities in the five country experiences is provided in Table 55, indicating those activities that are to receive priority.

Table 55: Activities Eligible for Financing from the Road Funds
in the Central Asia Regional Economic Cooperation Region

Activity	AZE	KGZ	MON	PAK	UZB[a]
Winter + summer maintenance	++	+	++	++	+
Routine maintenance/current repair	++	+	++	++	+
Emergency maintenance/emergency repair	++	+	++	++	+
Periodic maintenance/midterm repair	++	+	+	++	+
Rehabilitation/capital repair	++	+	+	+	+
Inspections and asset management	+	+	+	+	+
Operation of road fund secretariat	-	+	-	-	+
Toll plazas	-	+	+	+ (<2.5%)	-
Operation of road agency	-	+	-	-	+
Equipment procurement	-	+	+ (<10%)	-	+
Safety improvements	-	+	+	+ (<5%)	+
Geometric improvements	-	+	-	+ (<6%)	+

continued on next page

Table 55 continued

Activity	AZE	KGZ	MON	PAK	UZB[a]
Roadside facilities and services	-	+	-	+ (<1.5%)	+
Design	-	+	-	-	+
(Re)construction	-	+	-	-	+
Loan repayments	-	+	-	-	-

++ = eligible with priority, + = eligible, - = not allowed, (X%) = maximum percentage of road fund budget to be spent on activity, AZE = Azerbaijan, KGZ = Kyrgyz Republic, MON = Mongolia, PAK = Pakistan, UZB = Uzbekistan.

[a] Refers to the Republican Road Fund that existed previously in Uzbekistan. For the current Republican Trust Fund, the eligible activities are not clearly defined although it would appear that they remain the same.

Source: Author.

Maintenance and repair. The emphasis of most road funds tends to lie on the financing of maintenance and repair of existing roads. This includes winter and off-carriageway summer maintenance, minor repairs to the pavement and structures (current repair), renewal of the wearing course (periodic maintenance or midterm repair), renewal of the road pavement and repairs to the road base (rehabilitation or capital repair), and emergency repairs after damages caused by unforeseen events (emergency maintenance or emergency repair). These activities are rightly included in all road funds, as they are essential for ensuring that a road remains in good to fair condition throughout its life span. These activities are required for all roads at some point in their life span, and need to be carried out in some part of the road network every year. Therefore, it makes sense to finance these activities through a dedicated road fund, and to earmark specific road user charges for this purpose.

In all five country experiences reviewed in this document, the road funds cover all road maintenance and repair activities. There is a risk that a considerable portion of available funding is allocated to rehabilitation, especially where there is a serious maintenance backlog and a large portion of the network is in poor condition. This leaves insufficient funds for routine and periodic maintenance, subjecting roads in good and fair condition to accelerated deterioration and leading to an increased need for costly rehabilitation in the future. To ensure efficient and effective use of road fund financing, priority should be given to routine and periodic maintenance (maintenance, current repair, and midterm repair). Rehabilitation should be given a lower priority and should be financed only if funding allows for this.

Some road funds, therefore, define priorities or sequences in the allocation of road fund financing, or set limits to the percentage of funding that may be allocated to rehabilitation. The road fund regulations in Mongolia, for instance, give specific priority to maintenance, current repair, and midterm repair over capital repair, although very little midterm repair is carried out in practice.

Road asset management system. Rather than setting rigid priorities or limits regarding funding allocations to specific activities, a preferable approach is to use a RAMS to determine priorities. A RAMS tends to make use of economic criteria to prioritize those roads and activities that have the highest economic benefits per unit of funding. This tends to prioritize routine and periodic maintenance as these activities have high economic returns, although the rehabilitation of roads with high traffic volumes may also receive a priority because of the significant decrease in road user costs that may result from improved road conditions. In Pakistan, for instance, the regulations of the RMA determine that first priority should be given to routine and periodic maintenance followed by rehabilitation, but the actual allocation is defined by using the RAMS that looks at the expected economic benefits of different allocation options. As a result of the use of the RAMS, over half of the available funding is allocated to periodic maintenance because of its high economic benefits.

Apart from the initial development of the RAMS, this also requires regular collection of inventory, condition, and traffic data for the different roads in the road network. An annual budget allocation is required to ensure that the data is collected and updated regularly, and that the resulting identification of treatment needs and priorities is appropriate. Many road funds allow the collection of data and the subsequent management of the RAMS database and the analysis of the collected data to be financed by the road fund. The State Road Fund in Mongolia expressly mentions inspections as an eligible activity, while in Uzbekistan the development and operation of a RAMS is specifically defined as being eligible. In the other countries, the operation of the RAMS is not expressly mentioned, although this can be considered to be included under more general activities such as operational costs in Azerbaijan and the Kyrgyz Republic. Although in Pakistan the RMA is managed by the same unit that is responsible for operating the RAMS and the operation of the RAMS is financed from the RMA, this is not expressly mentioned as an eligible activity for RMA funding in the NHA Code or RMA Rules. Ensuring the availability of funding for RAMS operation can contribute to the efficient use of road fund financing, and should always be listed as an eligible activity of the road fund.

Road fund operation. It is common for the road fund to finance the operation of the road fund secretariat if this involves an independent legal entity. This is the case for the new Road Fund in the Kyrgyz Republic, and was the case with the former RRF in Uzbekistan. In Azerbaijan, Mongolia, and Pakistan, the road funds are not managed by an independent entity, and instead are managed directly by the staff of the road agencies, which covers the operational costs involved (although in Azerbaijan operational costs are listed as an eligible activity for road fund financing). In the new Republican Fund in Uzbekistan, the management is carried out by a department under the Ministry of Finance, which covers the costs involved.

Toll plazas. In some cases, the road fund also finances the construction of toll plazas and other toll infrastructure and equipment. Whereas the actual toll collection may be outsourced, the construction of toll plazas is often carried out by the road fund. This is the case in Mongolia and Pakistan, and is planned in the Kyrgyz Republic. Although this is justified from a perspective of increasing the revenue of the road fund, care should be taken that this is only done in roads where the toll revenue is expected to significantly exceed the costs of toll plaza construction and subsequent toll collection costs. This is not always the case, and Mongolia has several toll plazas where net revenues from toll collection are very low (even becoming negative in some cases).

Road agency operation. Some of the road funds also cover the operational costs of the road agencies that are responsible for the implementation of the works, including equipment procurement for the state-owned road maintenance units under those road agencies. In the case of Uzbekistan, a separate fund has been set up specifically to cover the operating costs of the Committee for Roads and underlying road management entities, financed from earmarked road user charges. Financing the operating costs of road agencies and related road management entities through the road fund can be justified if these are not directly involved in implementation, only in management. In the five country experiences presented in this document, the road agencies are set up as separate legal entities, and as such are not directly financed through the government system. Financing of the operating costs of road agencies should ideally be organized as a contract, with clear deliverables and performance indicators against an agreed payment, rather than as simple budget transfers.

The situation is different where such entities are involved in implementation of works. In this case, their operational costs should be covered in the implementation contracts signed with them, and should not be financed separately. This is evident especially in the case of equipment procurement, which is financed by the road funds in Azerbaijan, the Kyrgyz Republic, Mongolia, and Uzbekistan. These countries carry out maintenance and current repairs through state-owned maintenance units, with equipment provided to these units separately from the funding allocations for implementation of the maintenance and current repairs. In Uzbekistan, there is a move toward the commercialization of the state-owned maintenance enterprises, with all costs to be covered under the annual contracts with these enterprises (meaning that equipment will no longer be provided separately). This is a preferable approach, improving transparency regarding the use of road fund financing and allowing the performance of state-owned maintenance units and private sector contractors to be more easily compared. In Pakistan, all maintenance and repair activities are outsourced to the private sector, and equipment provision is dealt with by the private sector contractors and covered under the contract amounts.

Allocation of road fund financing to road agency operations should be limited to management costs, either through a separate management contract or as an overhead cost on top of each implementation contract. Actual implementation costs of works should be fully covered in the contracts signed with state-owned implementation units or with the private sector contractors, increasing transparency regarding the actual costs of works implementation.

Road improvements. Several road funds also finance road improvements, ranging from safety improvements and geometric improvements over short sections to full-scale construction and reconstruction of roads, structures and roadside facilities, and even the repayment of loans taken out for these purposes. Although the financing of spot improvements to improve safety or geometry from the road fund can be justified, this should always be limited to short sections and a small portion of the road fund budget. It is common to set limits to the amount of funding that may be allocated to these activities, as is the case in Pakistan.

The use of the road fund financing for full-scale construction and reconstruction works, including large-scale rehabilitation programs to address maintenance backlogs, is not considered appropriate. The high costs of such works put a very heavy burden on the road fund, and jeopardize the funding allocation to maintenance and repair. Road construction works can also be more easily postponed if funding is urgently needed elsewhere (e.g., during the COVID-19 pandemic), and that flexibility is lost when funding is earmarked for a road fund. For road maintenance and repair, the postponement of works leads to accelerated deterioration and a rapid increase in costs, and the reallocation of funding, therefore, should be avoided. There is also a common understanding that the development of the road network should not necessarily be financed fully through road user charges, as is the case with maintenance and repair, and that it should be financed instead by the wider population that benefits from the existence of these roads. Therefore, common approaches to financing of (re)construction and large-scale rehabilitation projects and programs tend to involve budget allocations, issuing of government bonds, development partner funding, or PPPs. These options are more suitable for financing such one-time investments, with subsequent maintenance and repair of those roads to be financed through a road fund and earmarked road user charges.

The current Republican Fund in Uzbekistan introduces such a separation in funding sources, with road improvements to be financed from state budget allocations or allocations from the Fund for Reconstruction and Development. In the case of the Kyrgyz Republic, the new Road Fund is expected to finance both maintenance and repair, as well as construction and reconstruction, without setting any limits or separating sources of funding. Expected revenues are insufficient to even cover maintenance and repair needs, and any allocations to (re)construction, therefore, will be at the expense of road maintenance and repair. The road funds in Azerbaijan, Mongolia, and Pakistan are all limited to financing maintenance and repair (the 2017 Law on Roads actually changed the scope of the State Road Fund in Mongolia to exclude the financing of construction and reconstruction).

Management Structure

Where first-generation road funds were set up as simple treasury accounts managed by the Ministry of Finance or directly by road agencies, second-generation road funds aimed to improve transparency and accountability by establishing dedicated road fund secretariats and road fund boards with representatives from different ministries and even from road users. The reason for this was that many first-generation road funds suffered from political interference and poor use of funding, with weak accountability and transparency. The creation of the road funds and the earmarking of specific revenues meant that approval regarding the use of funding was shifted from the Parliament (as part of the annual budget approval) to the road fund. If the road fund was managed directly by the road agency, this made the road agency directly responsible for determining the budget allocations to itself. Generally, the approval by the Ministry of Finance of annual work plans was still required, but this still limited the approval process to only two ministries. The second-generation road funds and their road fund boards aimed to improve this situation, ensuring that additional ministries and local governments would be involved, and including representatives from important road user organizations to ensure that their needs and priorities were properly reflected in the budget approval process as well as in setting the road user charge rates. In the second-generation road funds, the road fund secretariat and board are responsible for the financial management of the road fund, while the responsibility for the technical implementation remains with the road agency. Such a division of responsibilities is an important aspect of a successful road fund.

The eligible activities for financing by the road fund should be limited to road maintenance and repair, excluding (re)construction and large-scale rehabilitation programs. Localized geometric improvements and safety measures may be financed, but should be restricted. The road fund should also support the operation of the secretariat, the collection of revenues, and the use of a road asset management system.

The five country experiences include various approaches to road fund management. In Azerbaijan and Mongolia, the road fund is managed directly by the road agency, with approval of their annual work plans by the Ministry of Finance (Mongolia has a Road Board with representatives of road users, but this has a monitoring role only). In Pakistan, the road fund is also managed directly by the road agency, but revenues are off-budget and collected directly by the road agency, and the use of funding is approved directly by committees and boards consisting of representatives of the road agency and its parent ministry. In the case of the new Republican Fund in Uzbekistan, the road fund is managed by a department under the Ministry of Finance, but the annual work plan is prepared by the road agency and approved by the Cabinet of Ministers. In the former RRF in Uzbekistan and in the new Road Fund in the Kyrgyz Republic, the management was separated from the road agency and an independent legal entity was established (although in the Kyrgyz Republic it was placed under the same parent ministry as the road agency), while the approval of annual work plans is by a separate board with representatives from different ministries (and in the Kyrgyz Republic also representatives of road users), in line with second-generation road funds.

Road fund boards do not exist in all cases and, where they do, their membership is often limited. Azerbaijan and the current Republican Fund in Uzbekistan do not have road fund boards, and approval of work plans is the responsibility of, respectively, the Ministry of Finance or the Cabinet of Ministers. Pakistan and Mongolia have road fund boards, but these only have representation of the road agency and the parent ministry (in the case of Mongolia, the Ministry of Finance also needs to approve the annual work plan). Only in the case of the new Road Fund in the Kyrgyz Republic and the former RRF in Uzbekistan was a road fund board established to approve the use of road fund financing and to propose the rates for earmarked road user charges. Only in the Kyrgyz Republic does the road fund board also include road user representatives.

Table 56: Road Fund Management in the Central Asia Regional Economic Cooperation Region

Representation	AZE	KGZ	MON	PAK	UZB[a]	UZB[b]
Road fund secretariat	+	+	+	+	+	+
Road agency	+	–	+	+	–	–
Ministry of Finance	–	–	–	–	–	+
Independent legal entity	–	+	–	–	+	–
Approval by road fund board	–	+	+	+	+	–
Road agency representatives	–	–	+	+	+	–
Parent ministry representatives	–	+	+	+	+	–
Other ministry representatives	–	+	–	–	+	–
Road user representatives	–	+	–	–	–	–
Approval by Ministry of Finance	+	–	+	–	–	+

AZE = Azerbaijan, KGZ = Kyrgyz Republic, MON = Mongolia, PAK = Pakistan, UZB = Uzbekistan.
[a] Refers to the Republican Road Fund that existed previously.
[b] Refers to the current Republican Fund.
Source: Author.

It is strongly recommended to set up the road fund secretariat as an independent entity, either under the Ministry of Finance or directly under the Cabinet of Ministers. Where this is not considered acceptable by government, the road fund should be managed directly by the Ministry of Finance rather than the road agency or its parent ministry, ensuring a clear division between financial management of the road fund, and technical management of works planning and implementation. Annual work plans form the area of intersection, where planned works are linked to available funding. Whereas these plans may be prepared by the road agency according to agreed technical and financial procedures, and reviewed by the road fund secretariat to ensure compliance with these procedures, the final approval of the work plans should involve a road fund board with wide representation of both government and road users. Only in this way can proper transparency and efficient use of funds be ensured. A possible management structure is presented in Figure 18.

Road funds should have a secretariat that is independent from the road agency and its parent ministry. The road fund should be managed by a road fund board with representation from other ministries as well as road user organizations.

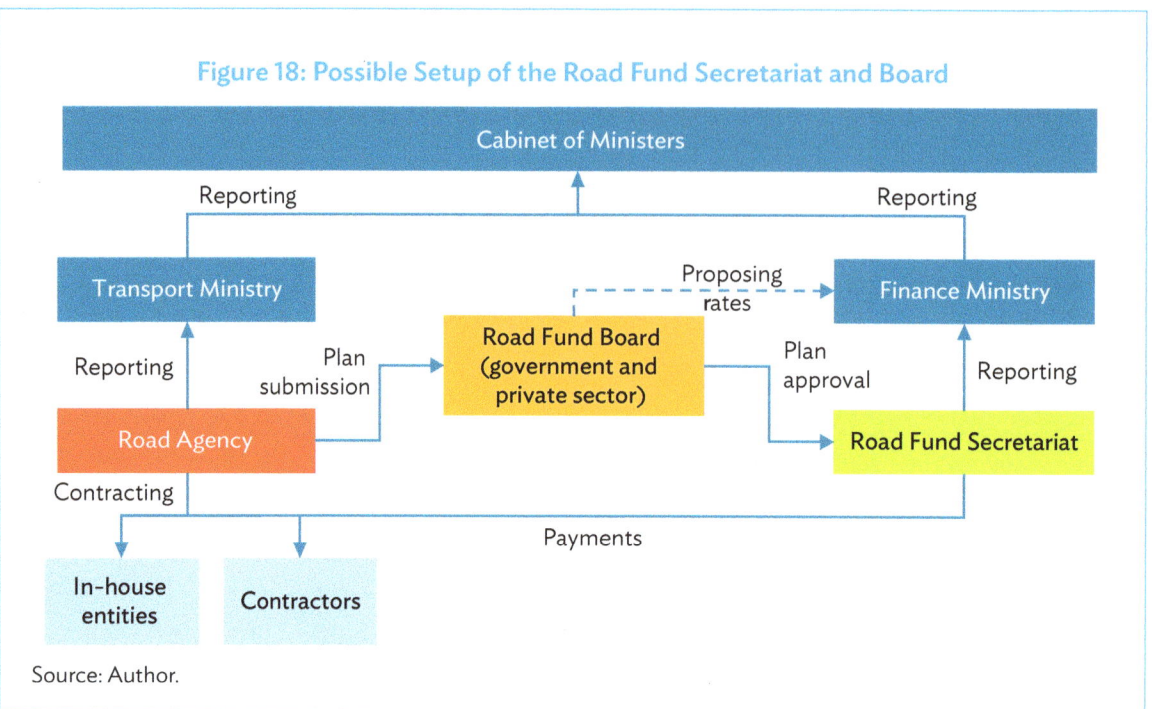

Figure 18: Possible Setup of the Road Fund Secretariat and Board

Source: Author.

Funding Approval and Allocation

The proposed division of responsibilities for financial management of the road fund and technical management of implementation has implications for the process of planning, budget approval, and implementation.

Preparation of the annual work plan. The road agency is best placed to prepare the draft annual work plan to be financed by the road fund. It has data regarding the status, condition, and usage of the road network, and can use that data to determine needs and priorities. Ideally, it should make use of a RAMS to help it to identify needs and priorities, but also to further optimize the use of available funding. Based on the draft annual work plan and related cost estimates, a budget request may be prepared. This should match the expected revenue of the road fund. The annual work plans may be complemented by rolling multiannual plans to show the needs and planned activities over a longer period, indicating the impacts of road fund revenue levels (and thus of different road user charge rates) on the future condition of the road network. This can help in determining the need for adjusting the road user charge rates, and in determining if additional revenue is required in the form of complementary road user charges, government budget allocations, or development partner financing. Here too, the RAMS can be helpful in estimating the impacts of different funding levels on future network conditions and on road user costs to the economy.

In all five country experiences reviewed in this document, the annual work plans were prepared by the road agencies. The only exception is the former RRF in Uzbekistan, which at some point became responsible for planning capital works, thus creating a parallel capacity to that of the road agency. Under the new Republican Fund, responsibility for planning is back with the road agency, and the road fund secretariat is only responsible for financial management. In Azerbaijan, Mongolia, and Pakistan, the road fund secretariat forms part of the road agency, and these responsibilities are mixed together. In the Kyrgyz Republic, the road fund secretariat is an entity independent from the road agency (albeit under the same parent ministry), and the exact procedures for preparing annual work plans still need to be defined.

Approval of the annual work plan. The draft annual work plan is generally submitted to the road fund secretariat, which will review it and confirm its compliance with the road fund requirements regarding eligible activities, eligible roads, etc. It will then submit it to the road fund board together with the secretariat's observations. The road fund board is ultimately responsible for approving the annual work plan and the allocation of the road fund financing. The inclusion of representatives from other ministries and from road user organizations will ensure that different views and needs are properly reflected in the final annual work plan. Where a RAMS is used to justify the draft work plan, the adjustments are likely to be minimal and will focus largely on additional criteria such as ensuring proper access to remote areas of the country, ensuring sufficient capacity of high traffic roads, and balancing contract packages with existing implementation capacities. Where a RAMS is not used in preparing the draft work plan, priorities may be more subjective, and it may be harder to justify these to the road fund board.

Of the five countries included in this review, the Kyrgyz Republic, Pakistan, and the former RRF in Uzbekistan involve road fund boards in the approval of the annual work plans. In Pakistan the road fund board only has representation of the road agency and the parent ministry, and the views of other ministries and road user organizations are not properly taken into account. In Mongolia, there is a Road Board with road user representatives, but this has a monitoring role only and approval of the annual work plan is by the Ministry of Finance. In Azerbaijan and the new Republican Fund in Uzbekistan, there is no road fund board, and, respectively, the Ministry of Finance and the Cabinet of Ministers are responsible for approving the annual work plans to be financed from the road funds. This means that the process for approving the use of road fund financing is very weak, generally only involving the road agency and the finance ministry.

The use of a RAMS to prepare and justify draft annual work plans is also very limited. Pakistan is the only country using a RAMS as the basis for its annual planning process. This greatly increases the quality of their plans and has led to steadily improving road network conditions. Although Azerbaijan has a RAMS, this does not appear to be used as the basis for planning. The Kyrgyz Republic, Mongolia, and Uzbekistan are in the process of developing their RAMS, but these are not yet fully operational and are not yet integrated into the planning system and the preparation of annual work plans.

Implementation of the annual work plan. For the implementation of the annual work plan, there are three options. The first option is that the approved budget is transferred to the road agency in the same way as it would be in case of allocations from the national budget. The road agency is then responsible for tendering out the work or allocating the work to its in-house entities. The road agency is responsible for the contracting and related supervision of works, as well as for making payments against the successful completion of works. In this option the road fund simply serves to collect revenues from earmarked road user charges and transfer these to the road agency. This option has the disadvantage that it creates a parallel capacity for financial management, as both the road agency and the road fund need to have a financial management capacity. At the same time, neither party has a complete overview of the collected revenues and implemented works. The State Road Fund in Mongolia and the new Republican Fund in Uzbekistan currently operate in this way, and annual reports and accounts of the road fund only mention the revenues collected and the funds transferred to the road agency, without specific details on how these funds were used. Financial accountability regarding the use of funds then lies with the road agency, in the same way as it did when it received allocations from the national budget.

Preparation of the annual work plan should be carried out by the road agency, with subsequent approval by the road fund board. The road fund secretariat should be responsible for financial management, while the road agency should be responsible for technical management of works implementation. This division of roles should be extended to the making of payments, with contractors paid directly by the road fund against technical certification of completed works by the road agency.

The second option is that the road agency tenders out the works or allocates them to its subordinate in-house entities, but that the payments are made directly by the road fund. In this option, the funding remains with the road fund, and the only transfers made to the road agency involve operational budgets for the management activities. This option has the advantage of continuing the division in responsibilities between financial management and technical management of implementation. The road fund is responsible for financial management and makes the payments for certified invoices and prepares reports and accounts regarding the collected revenues as well as the expenditures for different works and activities. The road agency is responsible for technical implementation, including the tendering of works or the allocation to in-house entities, and the subsequent supervision and inspection of ongoing works, certifying the completed works and invoices. The Road Budget Trust Fund in Azerbaijan and the RMA in Pakistan apply this approach, although in these cases the road fund is part of the road agency. The Kyrgyz Republic is also planning to apply this approach in the new Road Fund, which has established the secretariat as an independent legal entity from the road agency. The division of responsibilities for financial management and technical implementation allows the road agency and the road fund to focus on their specific roles. This is the preferred option and is reflected in Figure 18.

The third option is that the road agency tenders out a portion of the works or allocates these to its in-house entities, with the remainder tendered out directly by the road fund. Generally, this involves road maintenance and current repair being carried out by the in-house entities of the road agency, and all capital works being tendered out by the road fund. The distinction may also be made between domestically funded capital works being implemented by the road agency, and capital works with development partner funding being implemented by the road fund. This option has a disadvantage that it creates parallel capacities for implementation of the works, as both the road agency and the road fund need capacity to supervise and inspect works. The former RRF in Uzbekistan applied this approach, with the RRF tendering out capital works, especially those with development partner financing, and the road agency *Uzavtoyul* carrying out maintenance and current repair through its in-house entities.

Financial and Technical Accountability

There is significant variety in the way the accounts of the road funds are set up in the five reviewed country experiences. The simplest option is a basic treasury account with the Central Bank under the Ministry of Finance. This involves a specific treasury account that is dedicated to the funding of activities that are eligible for road fund financing, and that cannot be used for other purposes. The road funds in Azerbaijan, Mongolia, the Kyrgyz Republic, and the current Republican Fund in Uzbekistan are set up as specific treasury accounts (in the case of the former Road Fund in the Kyrgyz Republic, the special treasury account was never set up and the revenue continued to form part of the general budget). Some countries also allow the funds to be deposited in commercial bank accounts where funds that are not directly used may accumulate interest. This is the case for the former RRF in Uzbekistan. In the case of Pakistan, there is no treasury account since the revenues are extra-budgetary, and all funds are kept in commercial bank accounts.

Table 57: Types of Road Fund Accounts

Type of Account	AZE	KGZ	MON	PAK	UZB[a]	UZB[b]
Special treasury account	+	+	+	–	+	+
Commercial bank account	–	–	–	+	+	–

AZE = Azerbaijan, KGZ = Kyrgyz Republic, MON = Mongolia, PAK = Pakistan, UZB = Uzbekistan.
[a] Refers to the Republican Road Fund that existed previously.
[b] Refers to the current Republican Fund.
Source: Author.

The road fund accounts are normally no-lapsable, and any unused funds at the end of the financial year are carried over to the following financial year. This allows a smooth continuation of funding activities, facilitates the application of multiannual contracts, and avoids funding issues in case implementation is delayed. Apart from the higher and more predictable funding levels, this is considered one of the most important benefits of road funds compared to annual allocations from the national budget, where unused funding has to be returned to the national budget. Of the countries reviewed, only the Road Fund in the Kyrgyz Republic currently does not have a non-lapsable account, and unused funds have to be returned to the Republican Budget at the end of the year (discussions are ongoing to change this).

Table 58: Lapsable and Non-lapsable Road Fund Accounts

Use of Unused Funds at the End of the Year	AZE	KGZ	MON	PAK	UZB[a]	UZB[b]
Returned to the national budget	–	+	–	–	–	–
Non-lapsable, carried over to next year	+	–	+	+	+	+

AZE = Azerbaijan, KGZ = Kyrgyz Republic, MON = Mongolia, PAK = Pakistan, UZB = Uzbekistan.
[a] Refers to the Republican Road Fund that existed previously.
[b] Refers to the current Republican Fund.
Source: Author.

Most road funds are on-budget, meaning that their revenues form part of the annual budget and are reflected in the national budget. The exception is Pakistan, where the RMA is off-budget, with revenues directly deposited in the RMA's commercial bank accounts, without passing through the national budget or forming part of the annual budget approved by Parliament.

Table 59: On- and Off-Budget Road Fund Revenues

Type of Revenues	AZE	KGZ	MON	PAK	UZB[a]	UZB[b]
On-budget revenues	+	+	+	−	+	+
Off-budget revenues	−	−	−	+	−	−

AZE = Azerbaijan, KGZ = Kyrgyz Republic, MON = Mongolia, PAK = Pakistan, UZB = Uzbekistan.
[a] Refers to the Republican Road Fund that existed previously.
[b] Refers to the current Republican Fund.
Source: Author.

Financial and technical accountability and transparency are important aspects of road funds. The initial first-generation road funds made use of existing government systems for reporting and accounting. This depended on basic reporting and internal audits, which are generally not published. Because of the decreased role for the Parliament in approving and monitoring the use of road fund budgets, this was found to be insufficient and strengthening of accounting and transparency was called for. The second-generation road funds, therefore, included stricter financial accounting requirements, including annual financial audits by independent third parties. They also included regular technical audits to verify that the works carried out using road fund financing had indeed been carried out and had appropriate quality standards. The annual reporting was also strengthened, including greater detail on revenues and expenditure, describing the works carried out with road fund financing, and including predictions on future road fund revenues and road network conditions. To increase transparency, the financial and technical audits and annual reports are made publicly available on the website of the road fund and the road agency as well as their parent ministries.

In the reviewed country experiences, financial audits of the road funds are often carried out annually. In most cases this is limited to internal audits, complemented by audits by the government audit office (Chamber of Accounts in Azerbaijan and the Kyrgyz Republic, State Audit Office in Mongolia, Auditor General in Pakistan, and Main Control and Auditing Department in Uzbekistan). The audits by the government audit office, however, are not carried out each year. Independent financial audits are only carried out in Mongolia and Pakistan, where they form the basis for the government audits. The government audits tend to be quite thorough, identifying various issues regarding the use of funding and the compliance with road fund regulations, although it appears that these issues are not always addressed. Increased attention should be paid to following up on such issues, and ensuring that the road fund reports how these have been addressed in subsequent annual reports.

Technical audits are hardly ever carried out. In Pakistan they form part of the normal auditing procedures and are described in the SOPs and implemented by independent consultancy firms. The regulations of the former RRF in Uzbekistan allowed it to carry out technical audits of the works implemented by *Uzavtoyul* and later by the State Committee for Roads, although these technical audits were carried out directly by RRF and not by independent third parties. The lack of technical audits means that there is little monitoring of the actual volume and quality of works implemented using road fund financing.

Annual accounting reports are commonplace in the road funds. In most cases, these are submitted to the Ministry of Finance on a monthly or quarterly basis, complemented by an annual accounting report on revenues and expenditures that forms the basis for the audits. In some cases, the road funds are required to prepare more detailed annual reports, describing the revenues and expenditures, but also providing information on the allocation of funds and the works carried out. In the reviewed country experiences, such reports are supposedly prepared only in Pakistan, although copies could not be obtained. Such annual reports go beyond the basic accounting reports, and also provide information on the roadworks themselves and the road networks that these works are carried out in. They provide information on road network conditions, and the suitability of funding levels for maintaining those network conditions and possibly improving them. Such information can be very useful to ensure greater transparency on the use of road fund financing, and to justify possible increases in road fund financing, but these reports are not commonly prepared.

Publication of audit results and annual reports tends to be very limited. Generally, government audits are published on the website of the government audit office, but are rarely available on the website of the road fund or road agency. Often, the road fund does not even have a website. These audit results only provide financial data, and often do not provide details on the type of works financed by the road fund. Such information may be included in the technical audits or the annual reports, but these are not published in any of the five country experiences.

To ensure accountability and transparency of the road funds, independent financial audits should be carried out every year, and should be complemented by government audits at least every 2 years. Issues identified in these audits should be followed up and should lead to penalties if not addressed in subsequent years. Technical audits should be carried out by independent consultants or entities every 2–3 years, ensuring proper control over the volume and quality of works financed by the road funds. Road funds should be further required to prepare detailed annual reports describing revenues and expenditures, but also providing details on the financed works and their impact on overall road network conditions, and the future network conditions based on estimated future revenues of the road fund. Most importantly, the financial audits, technical audits, and annual reports should all be published on the website of the road fund (this requires the road fund to have its own website) and the website of the road agency, and made publicly available to ensure transparency.

> **To ensure accountability and transparency of the road fund, independent financial audits should be carried out every year, complemented by regular technical audits. Detailed annual reports should be published on the website of the road fund together with the audit results.**

Table 60: Auditing and Reporting of Road Fund Activities

Auditing and reporting	AZE	KGZ	MON	PAK	UZB[a]	UZB[b]
Financial audits						
Internal audits	+	+	+	+	+	+
Government audit	+	-	+	+	+	-
Independent third-party audits	-	-	+	+	-	-
Publication on website	+	-	+	+	-	-
Technical audits						
Technical audits	-	-	-	+	+	-
Publication on website	-	-	-	-	-	-
Annual reports						
Accounting reports	+	+	+	+	+	+
Detailed annual reports	-	-	-	+/-	-	-
Publication on website	-	-	-	-	-	-

AZE = Azerbaijan, KGZ = Kyrgyz Republic, MON = Mongolia, PAK = Pakistan, UZB = Uzbekistan.

[a] Refers to the Republican Road Fund that existed previously.
[b] Refers to the current Republican Fund.

Source: Author.

ROAD FUND REVENUE

Where the previous chapter looked at the management of the road fund and how accountability and transparency could be ensured, this chapter looks specifically at the revenues of the road funds and the degree to which these are able to finance the funding needs related to the eligible activities. It looks first at the sources of revenue of the five road funds, by focusing on the three main sources of revenue: fuel tax, imported vehicle tax or fee, and tolling. This is followed by a review of the actual road fund revenue levels in the five countries, by comparing these to identified funding needs and providing recommendations on ways to improve the coverage of these funding needs in the future.

Revenue Sources

The road funds in the five reviewed country experiences depend on different revenue sources. The percentages of road fund total revenue received from different road user charges are presented in Table 61 and in Figure 19. The road funds reviewed in this document, as most road funds in the world, tend to depend on three main road user charges: fuel tax, imported vehicle tax or fee, and tolling. In Azerbaijan, the Kyrgyz Republic, Mongolia, and Pakistan, these road user charges together provide between 64% and 100% of revenue. In the case of Uzbekistan, the new Republican Fund does not have any earmarked road user charge revenues and the revenue sources of the former RRF are indicated. This depended heavily on a corporate turnover tax that was a common source of funding for road funds in former Soviet countries (this was referred to as the road tax), although this is not considered to be a road user charge and has been since abolished in the different countries in the CAREC region. These three main road user charges are complemented by several other fees, fines, and taxes, but each of these tend to provide only a small portion of the total road fund revenue.

Table 61: Revenue Sources of Road Funds
(%)

Road User Charge	AZE (2020)	KGZ (2018)	MON (2020)	PAK (2019)	UZB[a] (2018)
Corporate turnover tax	–	–	–	–	68%
Fuel tax	30%[b]	73%	28%b	–	–
Vehicle purchase tax/fee	56%	20%	56%b	–	27%
Tolling	–	2%	16%	64%	–
Foreign vehicle entry fee	3%[b]	–	–	–	4%
International transport permit fee	4%	–	–	–	–

continued on next page

Table 61 continued

Road User Charge	AZE (2020)	KGZ (2018)	MON (2020)	PAK (2019)	UZB[a] (2018)
Vehicle technical inspection fee	6%	-	-	-	-
Load and dimension control fee	-	3%	-	2%	-
Indivisible load fee	-	1%	-	-	-
Right-of-way usage fees	-	-	-	6%	-
Compensation for damages fine	-	1%	-	-	-
Traffic fines	-	-	-	10%	-
Simplified tax for transporters	2%	-	-	-	-
Other revenues	-	-	-	18%	1%

- = not existing or not earmarked for the Road Fund, AZE = Azerbaijan, KGZ = Kyrgyz Republic, MON = Mongolia, PAK = Pakistan, UZB = Uzbekistan.

[a] Based on the former Republican Road Fund. The current Republican Trust Fund does not have any earmarked road user charge revenues.
[b] These revenues are reported together, and the division is based on estimations.

Source: Author.

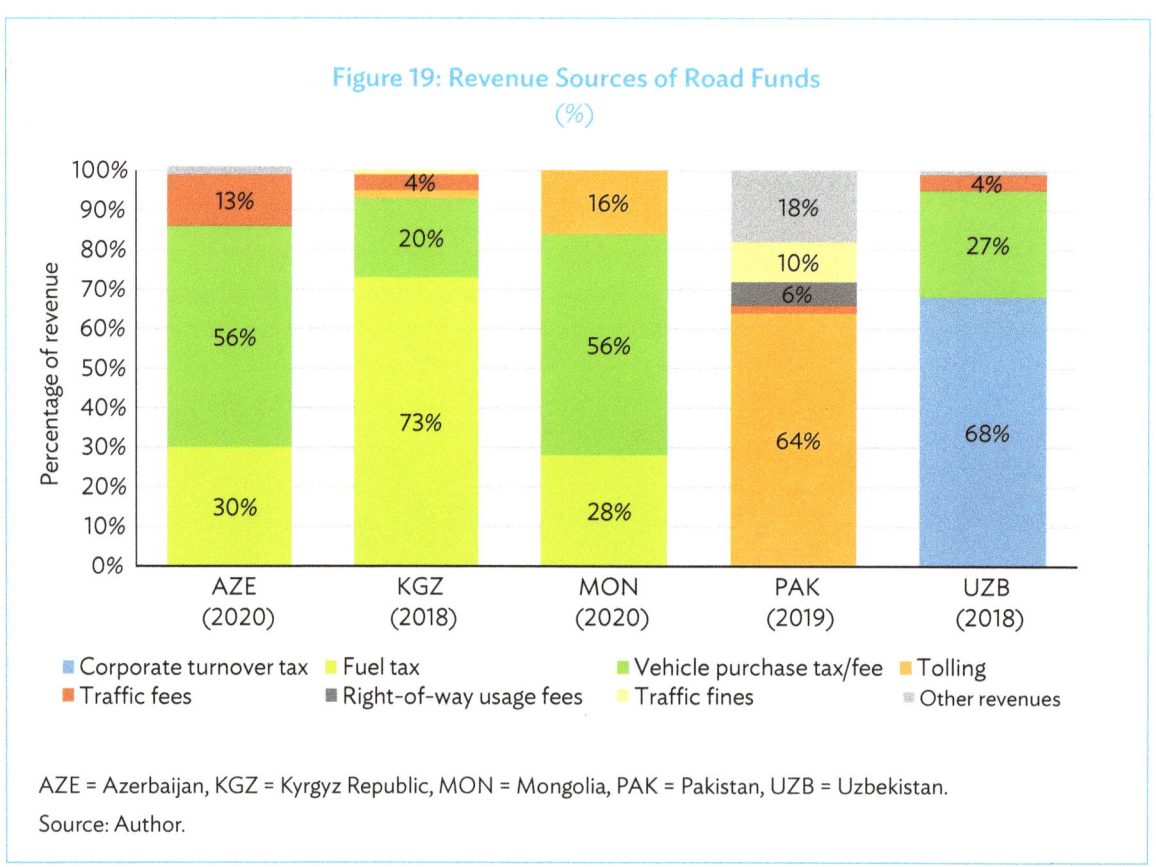

Figure 19: Revenue Sources of Road Funds (%)

AZE = Azerbaijan, KGZ = Kyrgyz Republic, MON = Mongolia, PAK = Pakistan, UZB = Uzbekistan.
Source: Author.

Fuel Tax

The fuel tax is the most common source of funding of road funds. This is because it is relatively easy to introduce with revenues increasing, as road usage and related fuel consumption increase. Road users who travel larger distances and use heavier vehicles are also charged more as they consume more fuel, further supporting the principle of "the user pays," putting the burden for payment on those that cause the most wear and tear to the roads. Collection costs are low, and are usually charged upon import into the country (generally collected by the Customs Office) or upon wholesale to petrol stations (generally collected by the Tax Office). Although the fuel tax is sometimes collected at the petrol stations, this is not a common approach. Depending on the fuel tax rates applied, revenues tend to be significant and can cover the funding needs in most countries. However, fuel tax revenues are often only partially earmarked for the road fund, with large portions continuing to go to the national or local budgets.

Fuel taxes also have some disadvantages. A major issue with the fuel tax is the difficulty of distinguishing between fuel consumed by road users and fuel consumed by other sectors (industry, agriculture, shipping, etc.). Although it can be justified to earmark taxes on fuel consumed by road users to the road fund, this is not the case for taxes on fuel consumed by other sectors. Some countries have introduced a parallel fuel distribution system for non-road use, adding colorants to distinguish the fuels, although this has not fully prevented misuse. Other countries have introduced subsidies to the non-road users of fuel to compensate them for the fuel taxes. Still other countries have only allocated a certain percentage of the fuel tax to the road fund, with the remainder going to the general budget and serving wider needs.

The fuel tax is the most common funding source for road funds because of the low collection costs and revenues that increase with road use. Attention is required for non-road-related fuel use.

Another problem with the fuel tax is that the tax rates in neighboring countries may not be the same, resulting in price differences at petrol stations. This can lead to road users crossing the border to get fuel. It can also mean that international freight transporters carry large stocks of fuel with them to avoid paying the fuel tax, thus contributing to the deterioration of the road network without contributing to its maintenance and repair. These issues can be countered by setting maximum volumes of fuel that can be imported in vehicle fuel tanks to avoid misuse, although the problem cannot be fully avoided.

The higher costs of fuel as a result of the fuel taxes also mean that transport costs will increase. This is relevant especially for freight transport, where the increased transport costs are added ultimately to the product prices with consumers paying the cost of the fuel tax in the end. As a result, many countries have lower fuel tax rates for diesel than for gasoline, even though the diesel vehicles are often heavier and cause more damage to the road network. As a result of such lower tax rates for diesel, diesel vehicles end up paying less than their share of damages. Therefore, it is preferable to set the fuel tax rates in relation to the amount of damages caused by different vehicle types.

The gradual shift toward electric vehicles is a major issue for the future of fuel tax revenue. These vehicles make use of the road network and cause wear and tear in the same way as a gasoline or diesel vehicle, but they do not contribute to the fuel tax revenue to finance road maintenance and repair. Currently, this involves a small portion of vehicles, but the number of vehicles will increase over time, and this will likely cause a reduction in fuel tax revenues in the future. This makes fuel taxes less suitable for future financing of the road network, although this is not an immediate threat, and fuel taxes can still be used in parallel to other road user charges that are applicable to electric vehicles.

Fuel tax revenues earmarked for the road funds in the five reviewed countries are relatively low compared to other countries around the world. The highest rates are in Pakistan, the Kyrgyz Republic, and Azerbaijan, but even these are low compared to international experiences. These involve fuel taxes that are not (fully) earmarked for the road fund (in the case of the Kyrgyz Republic, only 50% of the fuel tax is earmarked for the road fund). The fully earmarked fuel taxes in Azerbaijan and Mongolia actually have the lowest rates for fuel taxes in the five countries.

Table 62: Fuel Tax Rates
(US$/liter)

Fuel Type	AZE Road Tax	AZE[a] Excise	KGZ[b] Excise	KGZ[a] Excise	MON Tax	MON[a] Excise	PAK[c] Levy	UZB[a] Consumption	UZB[a] Production
Gasoline	$0.012	$0.065	$0.043	$0.043	$0.0056	$0.0047	$0.100	$0.0355	$0.0191
Diesel	$0.012	$0.042	$0.010	$0.010	$0.0007	$0.0073	$0.075	$0.0355	$0.0190

AZE = Azerbaijan, KGZ = Kyrgyz Republic, MON = Mongolia, PAK = Pakistan, UZB = Uzbekistan.
[a] Not earmarked for the road funds.
[b] Only 50% earmarked for the road fund.
[c] Pakistan has introduced a new fuel levy and is increasing it each month up to PRs30/liter.
Source: Author.

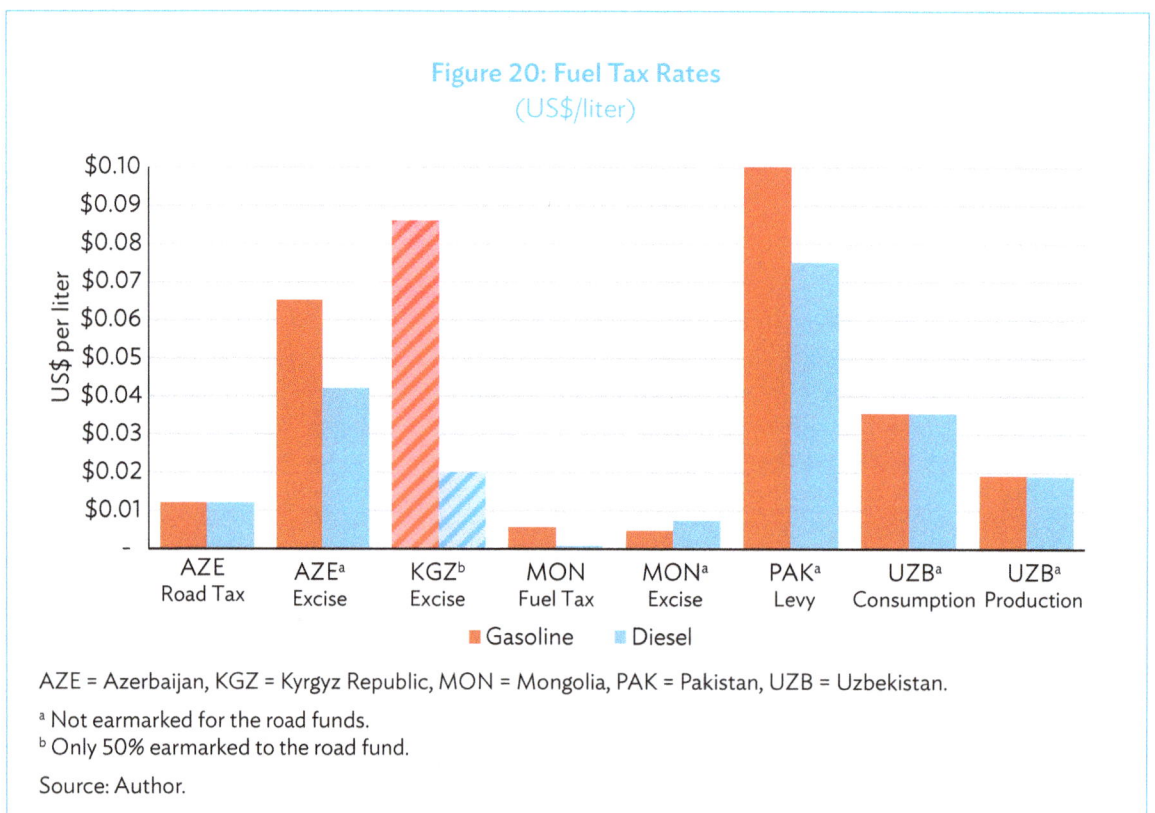

Figure 20: Fuel Tax Rates (US$/liter)

AZE = Azerbaijan, KGZ = Kyrgyz Republic, MON = Mongolia, PAK = Pakistan, UZB = Uzbekistan.
[a] Not earmarked for the road funds.
[b] Only 50% earmarked to the road fund.
Source: Author.

Only for the new Road Fund in the Kyrgyz Republic does fuel tax revenue form the main source of income for the road fund, even though only 50% of total fuel tax revenue is earmarked for the road fund. The revenue from the fuel tax in the Kyrgyz Republic has further increased with the doubling of fuel tax rates in 2020, and currently forms in the order of 85% of the revenue of the new Road Fund. In both Azerbaijan and Mongolia, fuel tax revenue forms nearly one-third of total road fund revenue. However, in both countries, the earmarked fuel tax revenue is a specific fuel tax, distinct from the main fuel excise tax that is collected separately. The revenue from the fuel excise tax in these countries is many times higher than that of the special fuel taxes, but is not earmarked for the road funds. Pakistan and Uzbekistan also collect significant revenue from fuel excise taxes and levies, but the revenues are not earmarked for the road funds in either country and instead go to the general budgets. In Uzbekistan, there are, in fact, two fuel excise taxes, each providing significant revenues, one of which goes to the Republican Budget, and the other goes to the regional budgets. This is the situation in most countries around the world that fuel taxes are already being collected and are providing significant revenues, but are not or are only partially earmarked for road funds or to the road sector in general. Given the fact that the fuel tax revenues form a clear road user charge and are already being collected in most countries, it is considered appropriate to increase the earmarking of this revenue to road funds.

Imported Vehicle Tax, Duty, and Fee

The taxes, duties, and fees charged on vehicles imported into the country also form an important source of revenue that is often earmarked for road funds. This may include a vehicle excise tax, a vehicle customs duty, or a vehicle registration fee (applied at the first registration after import into the country). Generally, these are collected by the Customs Office upon entry of the vehicle into the country. In the case of the registration fee for imported vehicles, in the Kyrgyz Republic this is collected by the Tax Office, while in Uzbekistan this used to be collected by the Ministry of Internal Affairs (the fee was abolished in 2022). This source of revenue has the advantage that collection costs are limited, as they are generally charged upon entry into the country and collected together with other customs duties and fees. The revenues collected from these taxes and duties are significant also, and cover an important portion of the funding needs of the road fund. The imported vehicle tax or fee can also be applied to electric vehicles, allowing it to continue to be an important source of funding in the future.

There are also disadvantages. This is an access fee rather than a usage fee, so road users pay it once when importing the vehicle, and subsequently can use the road network as much as they wish. As a result, road users that travel long distances and cause more damage to the road pay a similar fee as road users that use their vehicle sporadically. In addition, these taxes and fees are only applied to imported vehicles. In countries with their own vehicle manufacturing industry, such domestically produced vehicles will not be required to pay the excise tax or customs duty. The vehicle registration fee allows fees to also be collected from domestically produced vehicles, as these too need to be registered when they are first used on the road.

The imported vehicle taxes and fees also allow the use of new vehicles with lower emissions to be stimulated. This is evident in Azerbaijan and Mongolia, where older imported vehicles are required to pay higher rates than newer vehicles. In the Kyrgyz Republic and Uzbekistan, the rates are reduced instead for older vehicles, making it attractive to import second-hand vehicles even though these tend to have higher emissions. Most countries also apply lower rates for electric vehicles (and hybrid vehicles) to promote their introduction.

As can be seen in Table 61 and Figure 19, the revenue from the imported vehicle forms an important revenue for the road funds in four of the five reviewed country 63 shows some example tax and fee rates from the reviewed countries. The for five example vehicles with specific engine sizes and import values, allowing be determined and compared. As mentioned above, the rates will be different second-hand. Most countries apply specific rates that depend on the type of engine size, but in some cases the rate is set as a percentage of the import value

Imported vehicle taxes and fees form an important source of revenue that can be easily earmarked for road funds. This may also be applied to stimulate the use of newer, cleaner vehicles.

Table 63: Imported Vehicle Taxes, Duties, and Fees
(US$/vehicle)

Fuel Type	AZE Excise Tax	AZE Customs Duty	KGZ Registration Fee Inside EAEU	KGZ Registration Fee Outside EAEU	MON Excise Tax	PAK[a] Registration Fee	UZB[a] Registration Fee	UZB[a] Customs Duty
Motorcycle 250 cc ($5,000)	–	–	$230	$230	–	$100[b]	–	$20
Car 1,500 cc ($25,000)	$265	$600	$195	$500	$285	$500[b]	$750[b]	$3,000
Electric car 70 kWh ($40,000)	–	$600[b]	$180	$180	$145	–	$1,200[b]	–
Bus 6,000 cc ($100,000)	$9,400	$4,200	$435	$810	$5,425	$1,000[b]	$3,000[b]	$12,000
Truck 10,000 cc ($100,000)	–	–	$565	$910	$5,425	$1,000[b]	$3,000[b]	$12,000

– = not existing, AZE = Azerbaijan, cc = cubic centimeter, EAEU = Eurasian Economic Union, KGZ = Kyrgyz Republic, kWh = kilowatt-hour, MON = Mongolia, PAK = Pakistan, UZB = Uzbekistan.

[a] Not earmarked for road funds.
[b] Based on percentage of import value.
Source: Author.

Tolling

Tolling forms the third important source of funding for road funds. The amount of revenue collected tends to be significantly lower than is the case with fuel taxes or imported vehicle taxes and fees. However, the main advantage of tolling is that it is seen as a direct road user charge, and its revenue is almost always earmarked for the maintenance and repair of roads. Often the collected revenue is earmarked for the roads where the revenue is collected, although this is not always strictly the case and there is sometimes some cross-subsidization of other roads in the network. Tolling generally involves a usage charge, where road users pay according to the number of times they use the toll road and the distance they travel. In some cases, tolling may be seen as an access charge (e.g., vignette system, period-based contracts, flat rate tolls, etc.), where the payment no longer depends on the number of times the road is used or on the total distance travelled.

The main disadvantage of tolling is the toll collection cost. Operational costs of staffed toll stations can easily use up 20%–30% of collected toll revenue. This percentage increases as the traffic volume and toll revenue are lower. To ensure that toll collection costs do not form too large a portion of the toll revenues, toll roads should have traffic volumes of at least 1,000 vehicles per day. Preferably, tolling should be focused on roads with significantly higher traffic volumes of more than 5,000 vehicles per day. Where tolling forms an important source of revenue for the road sector, there is always a tendency to expand the tolled network and to gradually include roads with lower and lower traffic volumes. This has been the case in Mongolia, for instance, where toll collection costs averaged 30% of toll revenue in 2015, with collection costs in about half the toll stations exceeding 60% of toll revenue and even exceeding 100% in some cases (collection costs exceeded toll revenues). Great care should be taken to avoid this situation, as this results in a significant increase in road user costs, with only minimal improvements in available funding for road maintenance and repair. Although electronic tolling can reduce the need for staffed toll stations, there is still a need for specific infrastructure and equipment to be installed and for staff to manage and operate the equipment and monitor the toll collection. The use of electronic tolling also complicates access to the toll roads, as users generally have to register or purchase a tolling smartcard.

Another issue with tolling is that it is a general requirement that there should be an alternative route to the tolled road, so that road users can opt to use the alternative route if they do not wish to pay tolls. If the toll is set at a rate that covers only the maintenance and repair of the road, with a fair distribution between different vehicle types, it can be argued that road users of the toll road are only paying for the damage they cause, and that an alternative route is not necessarily required. However, these road users are also paying other road user charges such as fuel taxes and imported vehicle taxes and fees, and as such would be subject to double taxation. From this perspective, the toll road should provide something extra that warrants the additional payment on top of the other road user charges. This may be a shorter or faster route, for instance, with the option of paying the additional tolls in return for that benefit, or to opt for the alternative route without tolls. This is the approach that many countries have taken, defining in their toll legislation that an alternative route should always exist. Uzbekistan, for instance, is planning to introduce tolls only on new expressways to be built as alternative fast connections between major cities. Pakistan applies tolls mainly to its expressway and motorway network, although there are also open tolls on its highway network. However, other countries that also have this requirement of alternative routes are applying tolling to their general highway network. This is the case in Mongolia, but also Kazakhstan and the Kyrgyz Republic are planning extensive tolling of their main road networks to provide revenue for financing road maintenance and repair. In these cases, there are not many alternative routes and, where these exist, they are often of a much lower standard or are much longer. In the Kyrgyz Republic, for instance, the alternative route may be 3 times as long. Travelling distances that are 3 times as long over low standard roads may not always be considered a viable alternative route. Applying tolling to roads that do not have decent alternative routes is especially a problem for local residents along the tolled routes that tend to make extensive use of those roads. Although such local residents may be provided with free or low-cost passes to use the toll roads, this still introduces complications for them.

Tolled roads can have closed tolling with controlled access, where the road users enter and exit the toll road through a toll station, and the toll payment is calculated based on the distance travelled between entry and exit. Toll roads can also have open tolling, where access is not controlled, and toll stations are placed at specific intervals along the road. In the case of open tolling, road users can make use of the road without passing the toll station and paying tolls, meaning that only a portion of the road use is actually tolled. The payments at various toll stations tend to be fixed charges paid whenever the road user passes the toll station. Generally, the closed tolling is applied in expressways and major highways, which often run, more or less, parallel to alternative routes that allow road users to travel to and from places located between the formal entry and exit points. Open tolling is generally applied in situations where there is no direct alternative route and where road users need to be able to enter and exit the road at locations between the toll stations.

Toll collection can be carried out by government, either through their own staff (as is the case in Mongolia), or outsourced to the private sector (as is the case in Pakistan). In this case the collected toll revenue either goes directly to the road fund as an extra-budgetary revenue (as is the case in Pakistan), or it goes to the national budget and may be earmarked for the road fund (as is the case in Mongolia). In these cases, the collected revenue generally serves to finance the road maintenance and repair needs of the roads concerned. Also, tolling is often used to cover the initial construction or upgrading costs of the roads concerned. This may involve investments by government (including loans where needed), which are subsequently repaid from part of the toll revenue. This may also involve the so-called PPPs, where the private sector provides the initial investment for the road construction or upgrading, and receives (a portion of) the toll revenue to repay the initial investment and cover the costs of maintenance and repair, as well as the operation of the toll stations. Tolling is a common form of financing such PPPs, which range from full construction or upgrading of the road and subsequent maintenance and repair for an extended period (e.g., 30 years), to shorter PPPs that are aimed only at the maintenance and repair of the road (e.g., 10 years), and even to simple PPPs only for the construction of tolling infrastructure and installation of equipment and subsequent operation for a specific period (e.g., 5 years). Where toll revenues exceed the costs involved, a specific payment amount or portion of the toll revenue is paid to the government. Where toll revenue is insufficient to cover the costs, an additional payment on top of the toll revenue is made to the contractor. Several countries in the CAREC region are preparing such PPP contracts, and most of these will involve tolling. However, this should be seen as a very specific form of tolling where the toll revenue is linked to specific construction and performance standards to be complied with by the contractor.

Tolling should certainly be considered as an option for financing road maintenance and repair (and possibly even construction and upgrading). However, it is only applicable to a small portion of the road network that has sufficient traffic to ensure adequate revenue and to avoid that collection costs use up a major percentage of collected revenues. The need for an alternative route further limits the roads where tolling can be applied easily. To a large extent, the use of the toll revenue is limited also to the toll roads it was collected from. As such, this revenue is not available to the majority of roads. This means that tolling can form an important source of funding for the road fund, but only for a small portion of the road network. It will always need to be complemented by other road user charge revenues, specifically fuel taxes or imported vehicle taxes and fees, in order to cover the majority of the road network where tolling is not a suitable option. The reviewed experience in Pakistan is an exception because this involves a large network of expressways and motorways that are very suitable to closed tolling. Even in Pakistan, open tolling in the general highway network is subject to the same problems as mentioned above, and this is only increasing as lower-level highways are being transferred to the NHA by the states. At state level, road funds are also being introduced, and the lower traffic volumes mean that tolling is less suitable as a revenue source, and other revenue sources need to be earmarked. For a long time, Mongolia was dependent on toll revenue, but this could not cover the funding needs for maintenance and repair, and the recent allocation of fuel tax and imported vehicle tax revenues has resulted in an enormous jump in revenues of the State Road Fund. Therefore, the introduction of tolling should be considered carefully, identifying which roads would be suitable for tolling, and always complementing the tolling with other earmarked road user charge revenues.

Other fees, fines, and taxes

In addition to the three main road user charges described above, most road funds have also earmarked various other road user charges related to different fees, fines, and taxes. Generally, these provide only limited revenue, but they can also contribute to the total revenue of the fund and its ability to cover the funding needs. Some of the particular characteristics of these other fees, fines, and taxes are discussed here.

Vehicle inspection fees and permit fees. The vehicle inspection fees and permit fees include a variety of road user charges for domestic road users such as fees for the technical inspection of vehicles, for axle-load and dimension control of trucks, and for issuing permits for the transport of goods and passengers. These fees are all related to a specific service that is provided, and the fees primarily serve to cover the costs of that service. An additional amount is added to that fee, resulting in a net revenue that is earmarked for the road fund. The services provided are generally related to activities that governments want road users to comply with, such as ensuring the safety of vehicles through technical inspections, ensuring that vehicles are not overloaded or oversized, ensuring that transporters comply with minimum safety requirements, etc. Increasing the fees related to these services may lead to road users trying to avoid the fees, thus undermining the objective of the services being provided. This means that fees can only be increased slightly, and that they provide only a small portion of the total road fund revenues and an even smaller portion of funding needs. Therefore, whether such an increase in the fee is desirable needs to be carefully considered.

Foreign vehicle fees. A different situation is formed by the fees charged for foreign vehicle entry and for international transport permits. These serve primarily to compensate for the use of the road network by foreign vehicles and the damages they cause since these vehicles may not pay some of the other road user charges earmarked for the road fund. Generally, collection of these fees for foreign vehicles is carried out at the border crossings by the Customs Office together with the collection of other duties and fees. These fees are often earmarked for road funds. Revenues are relatively low, but serve specifically to compensate for damages caused by foreign road users, rather than damages caused by domestic road users that are compensated through other road user charges. The disadvantage of these road user charges is that they can lead to cost increases for imports, and are often reciprocated by neighbouring countries, also leading to cost increases for exports.

Right-of-way usage fees. Fees for the use of the right-of-way refer to fees paid for the placement of advertising or for the construction of facilities, such as service stations or roadside restaurants, within the right-of-way. These are commercial activities that are generally carried out by the private sector, with payments made to government for the use of the right-of-way. This revenue source is becoming increasingly important in many countries, and as such is providing increasing levels of revenue, which are earmarked for road funds in some cases. Some countries have issued specific legislation regarding the fees to be collected and the use of the revenues. Pakistan is putting significant effort into mapping the current use of the right-of-way, and properly regulating and collecting fees for usage. In doing so, it is facing historical uses and old leases that need to be regulated. Uzbekistan also collects

> **Tolling is often earmarked for road funds. However, the high collection costs and limited application possibilities make it less suitable for financing maintenance and repair of the complete road network.**

right-of-way usage fees, which are earmarked in part to covering the operational costs of the road agency, and in part go to the regional funds. This will become an increasingly important road user charge, both in terms of providing revenue for road maintenance and repair, and also ensuring proper regulation of the right-of-way.

Traffic fines. Several countries have earmarked traffic fines and fines for damages to the roads to their road funds. The objective of the fines is not specifically the financing of road maintenance and repair, but rather to motivate good behavior by punishing poor behavior in traffic. Revenues are often used to finance the operations of the traffic police, but any leftover revenues can potentially be earmarked for road funds. In practice, this can often be complicated, however, as the traffic police tends to fall under a different ministry. In the case of Pakistan, the National Motorway and Highway Police falls under the same parent ministry as the road agency and the road fund, facilitating the transfer of net revenues. However, revenues from traffic fines are not very predictable because they depend on poor behavior of road users, with revenues varying strongly from one year to the next. The fines are also intended to change behavior, and generally a gradual reduction in revenue is seen as behavior improves over time.

Locally collected taxes and fees. There are taxes and fees that are collected by local governments. Examples of such locally collected taxes and fees are the vehicle property tax, parking fees, and also in some countries the vehicle technical inspections (where these are not collected centrally). Revenues from such locally collected taxes and fees generally go to the local budgets, and as such are not very suitable for earmarking to a national level road fund. They can be earmarked for local road funds where these exist, as is the case with the regional funds in Uzbekistan.

Although other fees, fines, and taxes can provide additional funding to the road fund, these are often less suitable and their revenues are often limited.

Revenue Levels and Funding Needs

The road fund revenue levels for the five reviewed country experiences are presented in Table 64, which also presents the length of the roads that are financed through the road fund, allowing the available revenue per kilometer to be determined. This provides an indication of the degree in which the road fund is able to provide sufficient revenue for the proper maintenance and repair of the road network. Table 64 further presents the estimated funding needs for road maintenance and repair as identified by the countries concerned, together with the funding needs per kilometer. The latter may be seen as the target financing per kilometer considered necessary for the maintenance and repair of the road networks concerned, and depends strongly on the traffic levels, technical standards (e.g., number of lanes) and applied service levels. Lastly, the table shows the degree in which the available road fund revenue covers the identified maintenance and repair needs. Based on Table 64, the following paragraphs provide assessments by country of the road fund revenue levels and their ability to cover the maintenance and repair needs of the networks concerned, at the same time identifying possible ways of improving future coverage.

Table 64: Road Fund Revenues and Funding Needs

Road User Charge	AZE (2020)	KGZ (2018)	MON (2020)	PAK (2019)	UZB[a] (2018)	UZB[b] (2022)
Road network length (km)	13,671 km	18,942 km	15,249 km	13,570 km	42,869 km	42,869 km
Road fund revenues (US$ million)	$189.6	$35.8	$20.8	$258.7	$491.6	$223.3
Maintenance and repair needs (US$ million)	$200	$125	$60	$415	$433	$433
Road fund coverage (%)	95%	29%	35%	62%	114%	52%
Road fund revenues (US$/km)	**$14,000**	**$1,900**	**$1,400**	**$19,000**	**$11,500**	**$5,200**
Maintenance and repair needs (US$/km)	**$15,000**	**$6,600**	**$4,000**	**$30,000**	**$10,000**	**$10,000**

AZE = Azerbaijan, KGZ = Kyrgyz Republic, km = kilometer, MON = Mongolia, PAK = Pakistan, UZB = Uzbekistan.

[a] Revenue of the former Republican Road Fund from earmarked charges.
[b] Revenue of the new Republican Fund from regional government allocations.

Source: Author.

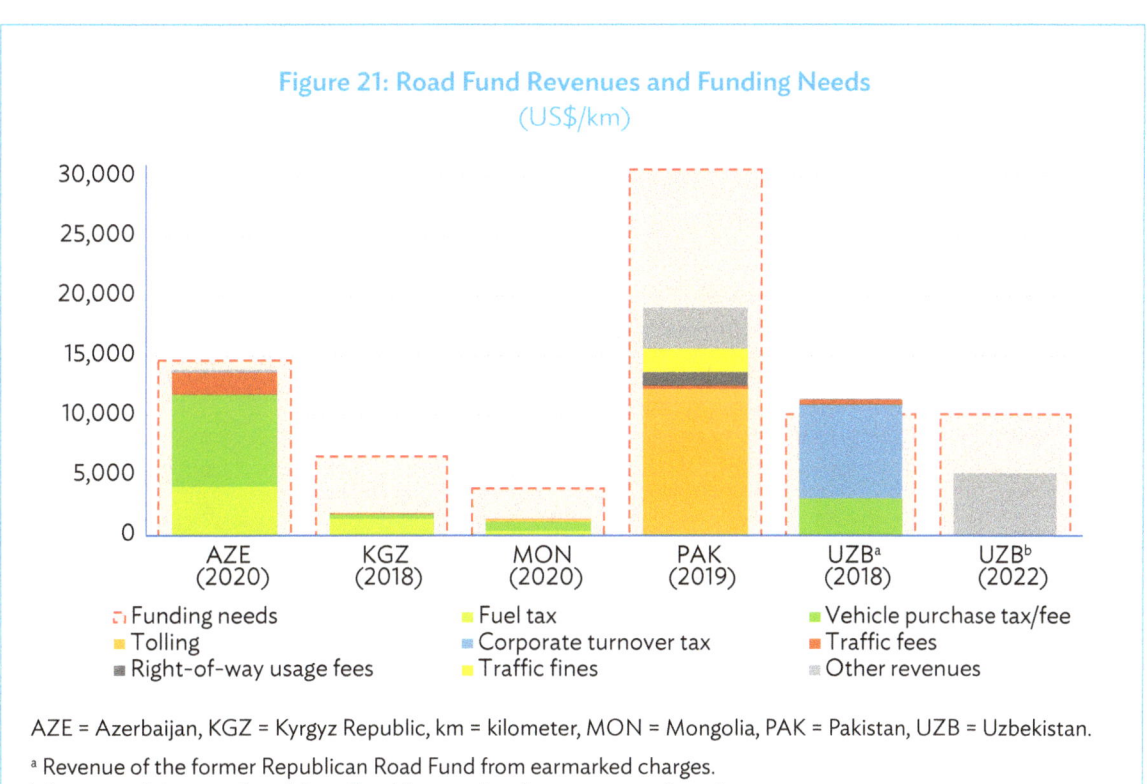

Figure 21: Road Fund Revenues and Funding Needs
(US$/km)

AZE = Azerbaijan, KGZ = Kyrgyz Republic, km = kilometer, MON = Mongolia, PAK = Pakistan, UZB = Uzbekistan.

[a] Revenue of the former Republican Road Fund from earmarked charges.
[b] Revenue of the new Republican Fund from regional government allocations.

Source: Author.

Pakistan

With $259 million in revenue in 2019, Pakistan has the highest road fund revenues for maintenance and repair, while at the same time financing the smallest road network. As a result, the available funding for maintenance and repair amounts to $19,000/km. However, the RMA in Pakistan finances a large portion of expressways and motorways with multiple lanes, and the available revenue per 2-lane equivalent road will be significantly lower and in the order of $16,000/km. The high-speed expressways and motorways also have higher standards and thus higher maintenance and repair costs than general highways, resulting in higher funding needs per kilometer. This is evident also in the funding needs for maintenance and repair, which NHA estimates to be in the order of $415 million, equivalent to $30,000/km. This funding level is considered very high, even considering that many of the NHA roads have multiple lanes, and likely includes backlog maintenance of roads that have not received adequate maintenance in the past or that have been transferred to NHA recently.

The current coverage of the estimated optimal needs is 62%. Coverage has been better in the past, and part of the problem lies with the highways that have been transferred to NHA by the states. These tend to be highways with backlog maintenance and with lower traffic volumes, and thus limited potential for toll revenues. This implies that revenues from other motorways and highways need to be diverted to these recently transferred highways to cover the funding needs. NHA will need to be careful in expanding its road network too quickly, as this jeopardizes the maintenance and repair of the rest of the network.

At the same time, there is limited room for increasing the road fund revenues. Toll rates cannot easily be increased, as toll road usage is already low and road users will make more use of alternative roads, possibly resulting in a decrease in revenues. Revenue from traffic fines is actually decreasing as the objective of better behavior of road users is achieved, and therefore does not provide much potential for revenue increases. Similarly, fees for axle load control cannot be increased much without risking that road users will attempt to avoid the weigh stations one way or another. The only financing source with some potential for increasing revenues is the commercial use of the right-of-way. Currently, the NHA is putting a lot of effort into mapping all usage of the right-of-way and ensuring that market prices are applied. This is resulting in some increases in revenues, but these are unlikely to provide the funding required. Another option for NHA and the government is to earmark additional sources of funding such as (a portion of) the fuel levy revenue or the vehicle registration fee revenue. This will be complicated, as the states will also demand their share of these revenues to finance the roads that they are responsible for. But this will ensure sufficient funding for the NHA road network, and at the same time provide more funding to the states and avoid the need for them to transfer roads to the NHA.

In terms of allocation of the available funding, Pakistan is doing well. Its RAMS forms the basis for the AMP financed from the road fund, and the RAMS has led to a significant shift in the way funding was allocated. Currently, half of the available funding from the RMA goes to periodic maintenance, and rehabilitation generally forms less than 10% of the budget, focusing on roads that have reached the end of their life span. This is resulting in efficient use of funding, and high service levels for the road network as deterioration of roads to poor condition is avoided.

Pakistan is ensuring the efficient use of its road fund financing through its road asset management system. However, funding needs are increasing as additional highways are transferred from the states and it is facing limitations in its ability to increase revenues of earmarked charges to match the growing needs.

Azerbaijan

Azerbaijan also has significant road fund revenue for maintenance and repair in relation to its network size. Its Road Budget Trust Fund is responsible for the second-smallest network, and collected $190 million in revenue in 2020, equivalent to about $14,000/km. The earmarking of various road user charges to the Road Budget Trust Fund, including a fuel tax, a vehicle excise tax, and a vehicle customs duty, ensures that revenue levels are considerable and can be increased as necessary. The estimated funding needs for road maintenance and repair amount to about $200 million, only slightly higher than current revenues, and equivalent to about $15,000/km. The estimations for funding needs are relatively old, and newer estimations may indicate a slightly higher funding need. However, the coverage is certainly high, with 95% of estimated funding needs currently covered.

Although there is not an urgent need to increase funding levels, there are ample options to do so. Small increases to the fuel tax rate or to the vehicle excise tax and customs duty rates can provide significant additional revenue to cover any funding gaps that may exist. However, as has become clear in earlier assessments, the problem in Azerbaijan does not lie with the level of road fund revenue, but with the use of the available funding. Earlier assessments have pushed for more funding to be allocated to midterm repairs (periodic maintenance). A comprehensive RAMS was developed, but does not appear to be used in preparing annual work plans financed by the Road Budget Trust Fund. Most of the available funding is allocated to maintenance and routine repairs carried out by the 103 economic societies under AAYDA, while midterm repair receives only limited attention. Without proper midterm repairs, funding is used inefficiently for routine repairs of roads in fair to poor condition, or for costly rehabilitation of roads that have been allowed to deteriorate to very poor condition. Improved efficiency in the use of available road fund revenues should be the priority in Azerbaijan. This will likely lead to a greater prioritization of midterm repairs, which will require that adequate capacity be developed to implement such works. Although some of the larger economic societies may have the required capacity to carry out such works, this may require the participation of private sector contractors to deal with the volumes required each year and to provide the necessary flexibility to work in different parts of the country.

Azerbaijan's road fund revenues are largely in line with its funding needs, but the allocation of road fund financing needs to be improved in order to increase the efficiency and effectiveness of the road fund.

Uzbekistan

In the case of Uzbekistan, the revenue of the Republican Fund is used both for road maintenance and repair, as well as construction and reconstruction. For this assessment, only the allocation to road maintenance and repair is considered. Of the $445 million allocated from the Republican Fund in 2022, $223 million was received from regional government allocations and allocated to road maintenance and repair, as well as the management costs of the Committee for Roads and its underlying entities. This does not yet include the operational costs of these entities that are financed under a separate Fund for the Development and Support of the Activities of the Committee for Roads.

The Republican Fund is responsible for financing the largest road network of the five countries reviewed here, three times as large as the networks in Pakistan and Azerbaijan. As a result, despite the considerable funding available for maintenance and repair (second only to Pakistan), the available funding is equivalent to only $5,200/km. This can be considered to be low, and does not allow proper maintenance and repair to be carried out. The funding needs for maintenance and repair are estimated to be $433 million per year, equivalent to about $10,000/km. This includes both high level highways that will require higher funding levels, as well as a very large network of local roads that will require significantly lower funding levels. A more detailed assessment of funding needs would require inventory, condition, and traffic data to be collected for the entire network.

The Republican Fund in Uzbekistan is a specific case, where revenues do not come from earmarked road user charges, but from budget allocations and other funds. Maintenance and repair of public roads are funded from budget allocations of the Republic of Karakalpakstan, the 12 regions, and the city of Tashkent. This results in a strange situation where the regional governments are required to allocate funding from their budgets for the maintenance and repair of roads that do not fall under their responsibility, and transfer this funding to the central government. At the same time, the central government through the Republican Fund is providing financing for the construction and capital repair of rural and urban roads under the responsibility of the regional governments. This exchange of funds does not seem very practical and needs to be changed. The allocations from the regional budgets through the Republican Fund to road maintenance and repair of public roads for 2022 are considerable and nearly at the same level as the previous allocations to maintenance and repair under the former RRF that was financed from earmarked charges. Actual revenues from these earmarked charges under the former RRF were significantly higher, reaching $492 million in 2018, and actually exceeding the maintenance and repair needs. However, a significant portion of the revenue was allocated to construction and capital repair and actual allocation to maintenance and repair was only $247 million in 2018. Apart from being lower than the allocations under the RRF, the current allocations from the Republican Fund to maintenance and repair are far from dependable, and it is unlikely that they will be easily increased to match the estimated funding needs, which would require a doubling of regional budget allocations to the Republican Fund.

While for road construction and reconstruction the Republican Budget allocations and the loans from the Fund for Reconstruction and Development are considered appropriate sources of funding, funding of road maintenance and repair requires stable and predictable funding, provided at adequate levels to match the funding needs. In line with the experiences of road funds around the world, this requires the earmarking of road user charge revenues to the Republican Fund, specifically for financing road maintenance and repair. The main funding sources earmarked for the former RRF have since been abolished, and new funding sources, therefore, will need to be identified. Uzbekistan already collects suitable road user charges that may be earmarked for the Republican Fund. This includes the fuel production excise tax with an estimated revenue of $150 million in 2020 that currently goes to the Republican Budget and could be (partially) earmarked for the Republican Fund. In addition, there is a fuel consumption excise tax with an estimated revenue of $200 million in 2020, but this goes to the regional budgets rather than the Republican Budget. Given that the maintenance and repair of public roads is currently financed from allocations from the regional budgets to the Republican Fund, even this road user charge may be considered for earmarking to the Republican Fund. In addition to these main revenue sources, there are smaller road user charges that may also be earmarked for the Republican Fund. This includes the foreign vehicle entry fee and the fees for roadside facilities that are currently earmarked for the Fund for the Development and Support of the Activities of the Committee for Roads. Earmarking (portions of) these different road user charges can provide predictable and stable funding for the Republican Fund and the maintenance and repair of public roads, while at the same time increasing the revenue levels to match the estimated funding needs.

An additional issue to be addressed is the allocation of the available funding for the maintenance and repair of public roads. As a result of the merger in 2011 of current repairs and midterm repairs, it is not possible to distinguish allocations made to isolated minor repairs (routine maintenance) from allocations to renewal of the wearing course (periodic maintenance) on the basis of funding allocation data of the former RRF or the expenditure data of *Uzavtoyul* and subsequently the State Committee for Roads and the current Committee for Roads. What is evident from the expenditure data is that the coverage of current repairs (including periodic maintenance) is very low, covering only 0.5% of the public road network or 12% of the international and national road length in 2020. In addition to this low coverage of current repairs, the expenditure per kilometer also decreased from $65,000/km in 2016 to only $30,000/km in 2020, implying a shift toward isolated minor repairs (e.g., pothole patching) and a reduction in the amount of wearing course renewals (periodic maintenance). This extremely low coverage of periodic maintenance is a serious problem for Uzbekistan, leading to inefficient use of available funding for isolated minor repairs in roads with older, deteriorated pavements, with the accelerated deterioration of these pavements leading to an increased need for costly rehabilitation. Uzbekistan does not yet have a RAMS to help it decide on the most suitable treatment needs or the optimal allocation of available funding, although, currently, it is receiving development partner support in this area. The development and integration of a RAMS should be considered an urgent priority, especially if road user charges are earmarked for the Republican Fund and proper justification is required for setting rates and percentages of the earmarked road user charges, and for justifying the use of the earmarked revenues.

Although (re)construction works and capital repairs (rehabilitation) are outsourced currently through competitive tendering, all maintenance and current repairs (including periodic maintenance) are carried out through the more than 200 maintenance enterprises under the Committee for Roads. These generally do not have the capacity to carry out wearing course renewals, which is part of the reason for focusing on isolated minor repairs. With the introduction of the RAMS and the expected higher priority to be given to periodic maintenance, the capacity to carry out such works will need to be created in the country. Although some of the larger maintenance enterprises can be made responsible for wearing course renewals or smaller maintenance enterprises may be merged to create the necessary capacity, this forms an opportunity to open up these works to private sector participation in the same way as has been done for capital repairs. If this coincides with increased funding availability through the earmarking of road user charge revenues, this does not have to affect the existing maintenance enterprises very much.

Uzbekistan needs to earmark existing road user charge revenues to the Republic Fund for the maintenance and repair of public roads, to create an increased and stable source of funding. The introduction of a road asset management system and the reintroduction of midterm repairs will aid in the efficient use of this funding.

Mongolia

Revenue of the State Road Fund in Mongolia has been limited to toll revenue for many years, providing just over $3 million per year in revenues. In 2020, the earmarked revenues from the gasoline and diesel tax and 20% of the vehicle excise tax were allocated to the State Road Fund for the first time, in the form of a state budget allocation. Revenue levels increased sixfold to $20.2 million, equivalent to a funding level of $1,300/km. This is clearly still very low, and only provides funding for maintenance and limited current repairs for part of the network. The funding needs for maintenance and repair are estimated by RTDC to be $60 million, three times the current revenue. This is equivalent to only $4,000/km, which is still considered low. With over half the international and state road network consisting of earthen roads, it appears that the estimated funding needs focus mainly on the roads with improved surfaces, resulting in funding levels for these roads in the order of $8,000/km. As the road network standards are gradually improved, the funding needs will become higher and need to cover the full international and state road network.

The toll revenues that have long formed the main source of revenue of the State Road Fund cannot easily be increased. Traffic volumes on most roads in Mongolia are low and, as a result, the toll collection costs form a significant portion of the toll revenue. Currently, the toll collection costs already form in the order of 20%–30% of the toll revenue, and this percentage will only increase as roads with lower traffic volumes are added. Expansion of the toll road network and construction of additional toll plazas are not recommended. The allocation of the earmarked fuel tax and vehicle excise tax revenues has resulted in a significant increase in funding. To increase the available financing of the State Road Fund further over the coming years, two options currently exist. The simplest option is to increase the percentage of the vehicle excise tax that is earmarked for the State Road Fund. In the Law on Roads, this percentage is defined currently as "at least 20%," and can thus be increased relatively easily without any major legislative changes. The second option is to increase the fuel tax revenue. This can be achieved by increasing the rates of the earmarked gasoline and diesel tax, although this requires an amendment to the Gasoline and Diesel Tax Law, which defines the rates and has remained unchanged since the issuing of the law in 1995. There is also a separate fuel excise tax, (a portion of) which could be earmarked for the State Road Fund. This would have the same effect is likely easier to achieve.

With the recent increase in revenue of the State Road Fund, it is even more important to ensure the efficient use of this funding. Several attempts have been undertaken in the past to develop a RAMS in Mongolia, and the latest attempt is currently ongoing. The RAMS will enable the government to better identify the necessary treatments and to optimize the allocation of available funding. Therefore, priority should be given to operationalizing the RAMS and linking it to the preparation and approval of the annual work plans for financing from the State Road Fund.

Mongolia needs to further increase its road fund revenues by earmarking a greater percentage of the vehicle excise tax. The new road asset management system can help justify the increased funding and ensure the efficient use of funds.

The increased funding availability and the use of the RAMS will likely lead to increased funding allocations to regular repairs (periodic maintenance). This received very little funding in past years, with only 18 km of regular repairs, equivalent to less than 0.2% of the paved road network, carried out in a period of 3 years from 2015 to 2017. Funding allocations are focused currently on maintenance and routine repairs carried out by the state-owned AZZAs under RTDC. These AZZAs lack the capacity to carry out regular repairs, which will require participation of private sector contractors. This will imply a major change for Mongolia, increasing annual procurement and supervision requirements, and should receive proper support from development partners.

Kyrgyz Republic

The Kyrgyz Republic abolished its Road Fund in 2018, and the new Road Fund will only become operational in 2023. The former Road Fund never really became operational, and earmarked revenues remained in the Republican Budget, with annual allocations to the road sector. This situation continued after the abolishment of the old Road Fund. Actual budget allocations to road maintenance and repair (including management and administration costs) amounted to $29 million in 2018 and dropped significantly in 2020 and 2021 because of the COVID-19 pandemic, increasing back to $25 million in the 2022 budget allocation. Earmarked revenues are slightly higher, reaching nearly $36 million in 2018. This implies an average funding level of about $1,900/km, given the public road network of nearly 19,000 km that needs to be financed from the Road Fund. This is clearly insufficient, and can only finance maintenance and limited current repairs in part of the network. A recent assessment of funding needs for maintenance and repair estimated that $125 million per year is required (this excludes funding to address existing backlogs), 5 times the current budget allocation to maintenance and repair, and equivalent to an average funding level of about $6,600/km. Although the public road network in the Kyrgyz Republic includes a large portion of lower-class local roads, this target funding level can still be considered to be low, and it is likely that an even higher level of funding is required to properly cover the maintenance and repair needs of the entire public road network.

Proper coverage of the maintenance and repair needs requires a significant increase in funding. Apart from excluding a significant portion of the public road network from receiving maintenance and repair, the only option available is to increase the revenues of the new Road Fund allocated to maintenance and repair. The road user charges that is earmarked currently to the new Road Fund provided $36 million in revenue in 2018. Since then, the fuel excise tax rates have doubled, and current revenue levels are expected to be in the order of $65 million–$70 million. However, this is supposed to finance both maintenance and repairs, as well as construction and reconstruction. Under such an arrangement, the allocation to maintenance and repair is unlikely to be much higher than the current budget allocation of $25 million. In order to ensure adequate funding for road maintenance and repair in the short term, the most logical option is to limit the eligible activities of the new Road Fund to maintenance and repair, and to exclude all construction and reconstruction works. The latter may be financed separately from Republican Budget allocations, development partner loans and grants, and other sources, but should not be financed from the limited Road Fund revenues. This change would allow funding for road maintenance and repair to be more than doubled in the short term, increasing the coverage to about 50% of the funding needs. This is still not satisfactory, but will mean a significant improvement.

The proposed revenue sources of the new Road Fund in the Kyrgyz Republic are insufficient to also finance construction and reconstruction. Although further revenue increases are possible, these will not be enough, and instead the scope of the Road Fund should be restricted to financing road maintenance and repair in line with other road funds in the region.

Currently, MOTC is focusing on the introduction of tolls for trucks travelling on public roads, and expects that over time this will provide about $35 million in revenue. This would ensure a further improvement in the coverage of the road maintenance and repair needs, reaching over 80%. However, this still does not leave any balance to be allocated to construction and reconstruction works or to rehabilitation of roads suffering under backlog maintenance. This further supports the recommendation to limit the new Road Fund to the financing of maintenance and repair of public roads, and to finance such capital works through other means.

Further increases in revenue may be achieved by increasing certain road user charge rates. The government has indicated that it does not wish to increase the fuel tax excise rate at this stage. However, the percentage of the collected fuel tax revenue earmarked for the Road Fund may be increased. This can provide significant additional funding without affecting road users. Vehicle registration fees may be increased, especially for new registrations of imported vehicles, but this is unlikely to provide the amount of additional funding required. The different fees and fines provide very little revenue, and here too a change in the rates will not provide the necessary revenue. Another option is to earmark revenues from other road user charges to the Road Fund, such as the customs duty on imported vehicles that could potentially provide an additional Som1.1 billion ($12 million) in revenues.

With the expected increase in funding for road maintenance and repair under the new Road Fund, it will become even more important to ensure that these funds are used efficiently. A RAMS was developed in the Kyrgyz Republic recently, but data has so far only been collected for 7,500 km of paved roads. Data collection is currently planned for the remaining paved roads and for 9,000 km of unpaved roads. This will allow a better assessment of the funding needs to be carried out and will form a proper basis for determining the treatment needs and prioritizing the allocation of the Road Fund financing to different roads. To ensure that the RAMS is properly used as the basis for planning, the Road Fund should make this a requirement in the approval of the annual work plan.